NEW POEMS BY JAMES I OF ENGLAND

NEW POEMS

BY

JAMES I OF ENGLAND

FROM A HITHERTO UNPUBLISHED MANUSCRIPT (ADD. 24195)
IN THE BRITISH MUSEUM

EDITED

WITH INTRODUCTION AND NOTES

BY

ALLAN F. WESTCOTT, PH.D.

INSTRUCTOR IN ENGLISH IN COLUMBIA UNIVERSITY

AMS PRESS, INC.
NEW YORK
1966

This Monograph has been approved by the Department of English in Columbia University as a contribution to knowledge worthy of publication.

A. H. THORNDIKE,

Secretary.

CONTENTS

INTRODUCTION

POEMS

PREFACE

THOUGH a more complete description and history of the MS. now published is given in the note following the Preface, a brief account of the nature of its contents seems at once necessary. The MS. itself has never been drawn upon for editions of King James's works, and so far as the writer is aware no critic or biographer has used it in his studies. None of the prose contents has appeared in print from this or other sources. Of the fifty-seven poems, twenty-six, or a little less than half — including most of the *Amatoria*, the long pieces addressed to Lady Glamis, all the poems referring directly or indirectly to political events in Scotland, and the excellent sonnets on page 39—have never been published in any form; and nine [1] more are now first discovered to be of royal authorship and properly arranged among the poems with which they belong. These, it will be seen, are among the more attractive and intimately personal of the King's verse, and such as by the nature of their contents were kept out of print during his lifetime. Of the remaining twenty-two, seven are found in *The Essayes of a Prentise* [2] and *Exercises at vacant houres;* [3] eight first appear in the volume entitled *Lusus Regius*, edited by R. S. Rait, Constable & Co., 1901 ; and the rest are in scattered sources not easily accessible. All of these — in other words, the entire verse contents of the MS. — are now printed, in the order and the text to which the King gave his final sanction.

[1] Cf. p. xiii.
[2] *The Essayes of a Prentise, in the Divine Art of Poesie. Imprinted at Edinburgh by Thomas Vautroullier. 1584.*
[3] *His Maiesties Poeticaall Exercises at vacant houres. At Edinburgh. Printed by Robert Waldegraue.* [1591.] This and the *Essayes* were reprinted in one volume, with a prefatory memoir, by R. P. Gillies, Edinburgh, 1814. The *Essayes* were reprinted by Arber, London, 1870, and again published, with the omission of *Uranie, Phœnix*, and other pieces, in a volume entitled *A Royal Rhetorician*, edited by R. S. Rait, London, 1900.

Thus, if one excepts the poems in the volumes of 1584 and 1591 (available in reprints) and the *Paraphrase of the Psalms* (still in MS.), the present volume forms with its appendices a complete *corpus* of the King's poetry.

The Introduction is intended not primarily as a critical study of James's verse, but as an account of his intercourse with poets and influence on the development of poetry. It is the product of research begun some time before the discovery of the MS. poems, and now condensed to make room for their publication. The writer has not felt called upon to attempt a complete or properly proportioned biography, though such a biography is still unwritten,[1] but has sought chiefly to present, in the light of newly discovered material, such facts of literary significance as have remained unknown or insufficiently recognized. The study is further confined to the King's relations with poetry, with only incidental attention to his prose writings, his political and theological controversies, or the vexed question of court influence on the drama. Matters of political and biographical interest (so far as they have no literary bearing) are for the most part treated in the notes at the end of the book, where an account is given of the King's journey to Denmark, his relations with Lady Glamis, the raids of Bothwell, and other episodes dealt with in the poems.

From a literary standpoint, the King's friendship with the Scottish poet Montgomerie constitutes perhaps the most noteworthy phase of his reign in Scotland, and it may be pointed out that not only the approximate date of the poet's death, but many of the details of his life, are altered by the information now accessible.[1] The King's early intercourse

---

[1] T. F. Henderson's excellent *James VI and I* (Gouphil & Co., London, 1904) is prohibitively expensive, and chiefly political in character. The biographies by W. Harris (London, 1753) and by Robert Chambers (Edinburgh, 1830) are both antiquated, and rendered practically worthless by the prejudices of the authors, and their efforts, in Chambers' words, "to make the book as amusing as the nature of the subject might lead the public to expect."

[2] Cf. the author's article on Montgomerie's biography, *Modern Language Review*, January, 1911, which calls attention to his service under James and Lennox, his friendship with Constable, and his death prior to the King's departure for England. This was written before the appearance of Mr.

with the English poet Constable and with the minor writers of his own court also calls for attention; indeed, so confined to the court was such poetical activity as existed in the period that a full account of the King's literary dealings might almost become a history of "school" poetry in Scotland in the last quarter of the sixteenth century. Later, during his reign in England, though the King's interests were chiefly in other matters, he was still surrounded by a coterie of somewhat amateurishly poetical friends and companions, mostly Scotchmen like Sir William Alexander, Sir David and John Murray, and Sir Robert Ker. Jonson, Donne, Drayton, and other English poets were friendly with the members of this circle, and there is some tangible evidence that changes in literary taste and fashions which were taking place during the reign were affected by court influence. In this connection an effort has been made to gather together such information as is available with regard to the extension of court patronage to men of letters. Accounts of the royal households and similar documents in the Public Records Office and the British Museum, as well as calendars of state papers and reports of the Historical MSS. Commission, have been searched for records of payments or biographical data of any kind. The results of this search are contained in Chapters V and VI of the Introduction.

In the preparation of the book, the writer has placed himself under many obligations, which it is difficult adequately to acknowledge. Gratitude is due especially to the guardians of the British Museum and the Records Office, for hospitality and courtesy which make his studies in London a pleasant memory; to Sir J. Balfour Paul, of Edinburgh,

George Stevenson's admirable edition of Montgomerie for the Scottish Text Society, 1910, which supplies new texts for the longer poems, and for the first time places his biography on a firm foundation. Mr. Stevenson's edition was not accessible to the writer before the text and notes of the present volume were in press, and quotations from Montgomerie are therefore from the earlier edition of Dr. Cranstoun (S. T. S., 1887). Chapter II of the Introduction, however, has been altered and corrected in the light of Mr. Stevenson's researches.

and Sir James Murray, of Oxford University, for information more exact and complete than a stranger could reasonably expect. The transcript of the epitaph on the tomb of Sir John Maitland was kindly supplied by the Rev. W. Proudfoot, of Haddington, Scotland.

Students who have worked at Columbia University will appreciate the author's debt to members of the English Department. In particular, Professor H. M. Ayres and Professor G. P. Krapp of Columbia have given assistance in linguistic difficulties which have arisen in the preparation of the notes. At all stages in its progress, the book has been under the supervision of Professor W. P. Trent and Professor A. H. Thorndike, and for such merits as it may have their guidance and practical counsel are largely responsible.

THE MANUSCRIPT

THE source from which the poems in the present volume are taken is a MS. now in the British Museum (*Add. 24195*), and acquired, as an inserted note indicates, "at the sale of Archbishop Tenison's MSS., 1 July 1861." A second inscription, perhaps in the hand of the Archbishop, reads, "Dec. 15, [16] 89. The Gift of Mr. Wright to T. Tenison for his library." Evidently, therefore, the MS. was preserved in the free library, the first of its kind in London, established in the parish of St. Martin-in-the-Fields by the Rev. Thomas Tenison, later Archbishop of Canterbury, not far from the time when the book was given. The donor was presumably Abraham Wright (1611–1690), clergyman and antiquary, whose death, it will be seen, occurred in the following year. The only later reference to the collection, so far as the writer is aware, is the following note in Dr. David Irving's *Lives of the Scotish Poets* (Edinburgh, 1804, Vol. II, p. 259): "Mr. Ritson informs us that in the library of St. Martins parish, Westminster, is a MS. volume, containing 'all the kings short poems that are not printed.'" Ritson died in 1804, but may have communicated with Irving when the latter was at work on his *Lives;* I have been unable to discover the information among his published writings. Dr. Irving presumably did not gain access to the poems, or he would have spoken of them in his criticism of the King's works.

The MS. itself consists of eighty-five folios, in the original white vellum binding, with ornate cover designs in gold inclosing the motto, "Domine salvum fac regem." Sixty-one of the folios are occupied by the poems, and a part of the remainder by tables of contents at the beginning and the end, specimens of the King's correspondence with

foreign scholars, and other short prose pieces.[1] On the
inside of the back cover the name Charles is twice written;
and on the fly-leaves are scraps of verse and the signatures
of Thomas Cary,[2] James Leviston,[3] and Doctor John
Craig.[4] The tables of contents, some of the headings of
poems, numerous corrections, and five of the sonnets are
written by Prince Charles, and Carey's hand appears frequently in corrections and in the sonnets now numbered
XLVI and XLVII.[5] The fact that some of the changes are
in the hand of the King indicates that he also went over the
copy.[6] The greater portion of the MS. is in a neat print-
like hand, the same as that of the Museum MS. (*Old Royal,
18 B XIV*) of the King's *Paraphrase of the Psalms.* The
copyist of the latter was a Scotchman, as is indicated by the
dialect of his marginal notes; and it is in any case more
likely that the task of transcribing the King's verse and
turning it into English would be given to one familiar with
the Scottish dialect, for example, either John or Thomas
Murray, secretaries respectively to the King and the Prince.

A possible theory regarding the formation of the collection, based on the signatures and the handwritings, is that
it was prepared in the King's household, corrected by James,
and again revised — whether before or after James's death
is not certain — by Charles and Carey. In 1626, Sir
William Alexander was delegated to "consider and review

---

[1] Cf. App. I.

[2] Thomas Cary, or Carey (1597–1634), not to be confused with the poet
of the same name, was a younger son of Sir Robert Carey, who was guardian
of Prince Charles and head of his household until he came to the throne.
Thomas was made a groom of the chamber to the Prince on his creation
(*Memoirs of Sir Robert Carey*, ed. 1808, p. 105), and retained the position
after Charles became king. On the latter's accession he was granted a
pension of £500 a year (*Cal. S. P. Dom.*, May 25, 1625).

[3] James Leviston, William Murray, and Endymion Porter, all grooms
of the chamber to Charles, received pensions of £500 at the same time as
Carey (*ibid.*). Leviston, or Livingstone, was knighted before 1629 and made
Earl of Callander in 1641.

[4] John Craig (d. 1654) was physician to James and afterward to Charles.
He succeeded his father, of the same name, who died in 1620.

[5] This description is in accord with the one given in the Museum Cata-
logue.   [6] Cf. footnotes, pp. 5, 10, 19, 25, 43, 53, etc.

the meeter and poesie" of the King's psalms,[1] with a view to publication, and an edition — the text quite different, however, from that of the Museum MS. — appeared in 1631. Charles may have also planned an edition of the poems, but decided afterward not to expose them thus to the attacks of Puritan critics. The corrections by the King, and the proper placing (in a MS. which now contains no blank pages) of the poems copied by Charles and Carey, suggest a date somewhere between 1616 and 1625. The care with which the collection is arranged, revised, and the pieces which had already appeared in print crossed through, makes it altogether probable that James himself planned to have it published; it may at least be accepted as a correct and final text for the poems which it contains.

Of these, the pieces hitherto printed (from other MS. sources) have already been roughly indicated in the Preface, and it remains merely to give a fuller account of the two collections in which most of them appear.

Nine sonnets — corresponding, in the order in which they are printed, to XV, V, VI, II, X, VIII, XI, XII, and IX of the *Amatoria* — are found in the *Publications of the Percy Society*, 1844, Vol. XV, pp. 32–37. They are arranged as a single poem, and form a part of a series of extracts, entitled *Poetical Miscellanies*, selected and edited by J. C. Halliwell from a much larger collection in a MS. volume, 12mo., owned at the time by Andrews, a Bristol bookseller.[2] At the end of the sonnets is the colophon, " Finis, Sir Thomas Areskine of Gogar, Knighte " — a signature which has served completely to conceal their actual authorship. Sir Thomas Areskine, or Erskine, was either the King's friend and boyhood companion of that name, who became Earl of Kelley in 1619, or his grandson and namesake, who became the second earl in 1639.[3] The variants in the Percy Society

---

[1] Letter of Charles to the Archbishop of St. Andrews, *Earl of Stirling's Reg. Royal Letters*, Edinburgh, 1885, Vol. I, p. 73.

[2] Halliwell's preface to the *Miscellanies*.

[3] It is possibly of significance that a complication of marriages placed the younger Erskine in the relationship of grandson to James Leviston, though the two were not far from the same age. (Cf. *D.N.B.*)

text, though frequent, consist wholly of obvious errors in transcription or printing, and it is altogether probable, therefore, that Erskine's MS. was merely a copy of the one now in the Museum.

A more important collection of James's poems is the one entitled *Lusus Regius*,[1] edited by R. S. Rait in 1901 from two MSS. in the Bodleian Library (*MS. Bodl. 165–166*). These MSS. are in the Scottish dialect, almost entirely in the King's handwriting, and contain many of his compositions in prose and verse. From corrections and marginal notes it seems probable that they were among the first drafts from which the Museum collection was prepared. Nine of the twelve pieces published by Mr. Rait, or all save the psalms and the prose, appear in the Museum MS. and are now printed. His table of contents follows, with references to the corresponding poems in the present volume.

I. Fragment of a Masque . . . *An Epithalamion upon the Marques of Huntlies Mariage*, pp. 47–52. The sonnet on p. 49 is not in Rait.

II. 'Ane Admonition to the Maister Poete to leave of greit crakking.' . . . *An admonition*, etc., pp. 40–44. The final stanza, following the sonnet, is not in Rait.

III. Sonnet to Bacchus . . . The sonnet referring to the death of Montgomerie, p. 37.

IV. On Women . . . *A Satire against Woemen*, pp. 19–21.

V. 'Bot be the Contraire I Reiose.' . . . This, with the stanzas properly arranged, is *Song I*, pp. 22–23.

VI. ' If Mourning micht Amende.' . . . *A Dier at her M^{lies} Desyr*, pp. 7–9.

VII. 'Gif all the Floudis amangis Thaime walde Concluid.' . . . *Ex Lucano libro quinto*, pp. 44–45.

---

[1] *Lusus Regius, being Poems and Other Pieces by King James Ye First. Now first set forth and Edited by R. S. Rait*, Constable & Co., 1901. This is an expensive edition limited to 275 copies.

Mr. Rait does not call attention to the fact that this appears in *The Essayes of a Prentise*.

VIII. 'This Lairgeness and this Breadth so Long' . . . *A Pairt of Du Bartas First Day*, pp. 54–56.

IX. On his own Destiny . . . *The Beginning of his M^{ties} Jurnei*, pp. 52–53.

X. The CI Psalm . . . Not in the Museum MS.

XI. 'His Maiesties Letter unto Mr. Du Bartas' . . . A letter in French inviting the poet to Scotland. Cf. App. I, IV, p. 60.

XII. Supplement to the Preface of the Βασιλικὸν Δῶρον. . . A paragraph explaining his attacks on the Puritans. Not in the Museum MS.

It will be seen that the titles in the Museum MS. frequently indicate the occasions or sources of the poems. Obscurities and breaks in the Bodleian MS. are also at times remedied in the Museum copy. The Bodleian, it is true, presents the poems in the dialect in which they were originally written; but it was the King's intention and it will be the preference of many readers that his verse, like his prose, should appear in the more familiar, not to say less uncouth, Southern language and spelling. The change is made without seriously affecting either the meter or the sense. Aside from the relative merits of the texts, it is desirable to have together in convenient form all the verse of the King not in *The Essayes of a Prentise* or the *Exercises at vacant houres*.

In printing the poems it has seemed advisable, even in the cases of the half dozen or more poems published in the King's lifetime, to follow carefully the punctuation of the MS. This, though scanty, is not seriously misleading, if one remembers that the pauses at the ends of lines are usually unmarked. In spelling, the long *s* has been discarded, and the scribal interchange of *u*, *v*, and *w*, and of *i* and *j*, brought into conformity with modern usage. In other respects, both spelling and capitalization (save in the titles) follow the original exactly, and have been verified by collation of the proof with the MS. Changes in handwriting are as a rule recorded, since they indicate the King's supervision, the authenticity of titles and corrections, and the extent of the alterations made by Charles and Carey. Corrections are in all cases followed in the text, with the original phrasing, if decipherable, indicated in footnotes; variant readings from printed sources are also given when they are of the slightest importance or when the difference is not merely in spelling or dialect. Comment other than textual is reserved for the notes at the end.

INTRODUCTION

I

THE KING AND HIS TUTORS

" Quæ tam docta fuit, quamvis privata, juventus ? "
— GROTIUS, *Poemata*, p. 64.

THE series of murders, tumults, and intrigues which
finally left the infant James an orphan in the hands of his
mother's enemies, gave the nobles and clergy of that faction
a rare opportunity for educational experiment. The result
was ironically unexpected, but even in the light of results
one cannot criticize the earnestness or wisdom with which
the experiment was undertaken. In August, 1569,[1] when
the King was but a little over three years old, four precep-
tors were appointed to take charge of his moral and intellectual training. Two of these, David and Adam Erskine,
lay Abbots respectively of Cambuskenneth and Dryburgh,
obtained their posts as kinsmen of the Earl of Mar, the
King's guardian. Both were of the royal household and
allies of Morton in the troubles of 1578,[2] and prominent
among the plotters against the King in the Raid of Ruthven
(1582) ;[3] but they are not mentioned as tutors in later acts
of the Council, and it is not clear that they were ever closely
associated with the King as instructors. The remaining
two, George Buchanan and Peter Young, were confirmed

---

[1] *Dict. Nat. Biog.*, from a document among Lord Haddington's MSS.
in the Advocates' Library. The tutors entered upon their duties early in the
following year, — "Admissus in clientalem regis, January 4, 1569 [70] "
(Young's *Ephemeride*, in *Vitæ Quorundam Eruditissimorum & illustrium
Virorum*, Th. Smith, London, 1707, p. 23).

[2] *Memoirs of Sir James Melville*, Bann. Club, p. 236.

[3] *Papers relating to the Master of Gray*, Bann. Club, p. 59.

in their offices by two subsequent acts of the Privy Council,[1] following changes in the regency. The form in each case was the same; the King's education in "literature and religioun" was to continue under "Maisteris George Buchannane and Petir Young his present Pedagogis, or sic as salbe heireftir appointit . . . agreing in religioun with the saidis Maisteris." The characters of all four tutors and of the widow of the Earl of Mar, who was mistress of the household at Stirling, are succinctly indicated by a passage in Sir James Melville's *Memoirs:* "The tua abbotis wer wyse and modest; My Lady Mar was wyse and schairp, and held the King in gret aw; and sa did Mester George Buchwennen. Mester Peter Yong was gentiller, and was laith till offend the King at any tym, and used him self wairly, as a man that had mynd of his awen weill, be keping of his Maiesteis favour. Bot Mester George was a stoik philosopher and loked not far before the hand. . . . He was also of gud religion for a poet." [2]

Buchanan and Young together were chiefly responsible for the King's training in morals and scholarship during the twelve quiet years he spent at Stirling Castle. The choice of the former was predetermined by his eminence not only in Scotland but in all Europe as a teacher, scholar, and writer. Though at the time of his appointment he had written nothing in the vernacular, he had a wide reputation as a poet and dramatist in Latin,[3] and as a leader of Protestant thought in politics and theology. His *De Jure Regni apud Scotos* gives a sufficient idea of the startling, though from a modern standpoint sound, political doctrines with which James's mind was fed during his credulous childhood. Written at the time of Mary's downfall, it asserts the accountability of a ruler to his subjects, justifies tyrannicide, and shows incidentally to what an extent radical political

---

[1] *Acts of the Privy Council of Scotland*, January 28, 1572–1573, following the death of Mar; May 3, 1578, following the temporary fall of Morton.

[2] Bannatyne Club edition, p. 262.

[3] Cf. Du Bellay, *Regrets*, sonnet CLXXIX : —

"Buchanan, qui d'un vers aux plus vieux comparable
Le surnom de Sauvage ostes à l'Ecossois."

thought was in the air while the first Stuart king of England was still an infant. Much of this teaching James absorbed, and it appears later oddly mixed with his own natural and, in his situation, justifiable views of royal prerogative. In later years, James usually spoke of Buchanan with respect. He told Scaravelli, the Venetian Secretary in England, of "the days . . . when my tutor, Buchanan, gave me instruction in the excellence of that government [the Venetian Republic]";[1] and he ascribed the correctness of his Latin pronunciation to Buchanan, "who is well-known one of the best Latin scholars in all Europe."

To the same influence James, no doubt, owed the beginning of his ambition to become a scholar and writer; some of his shorter poems, notably *An Ænigme of Sleepe* and *A Sonnet on the Moneth of May*, are similar in theme and treatment to Latin poems of his tutor, and it is quite possible that many of the classical ornaments and allusions in his verse could be traced to the same source. Yet in the final fixing of his literary tastes and of his character in general, the older teacher probably did not have so large a share as is commonly supposed. A letter from Buchanan to Rodolph Gualter, July 24, 1579,[2] refers to his increasing illness, and suggests that his relations with the King were already becoming strained: "I have now been from the court more than six weeks by reason of ill health; but as soon as I return hither, I will endeavor that the King shall steal a few moments from his occupations to give you a testimony of his favorable regard . . . and should I not be able to accomplish this myself, I will take care that it shall be managed by my colleague the pious and learned Peter Young." Buchanan at this time was in his seventy-fourth year; he speaks again in the dedication to James of his *History of Scotland* (September, 1581) of the 'incurable illness which had prevented him from carrying on the duties of instruction.' It is clear, moreover, from the

---

[1] *Cal. S. P. Venetian*, Vol. X, No. 78 (1603).

[2] *Zurich Letters*, Parker Soc., 1845, Second Series, p. 310. Gualter had dedicated to James his *Homilies on St. Paul* (1576).

statement of Melville already quoted and from numerous anecdotes, apocryphal or otherwise, that Buchanan, who as a member of the Lennox family had a special hatred for Queen Mary, extended his dislike to the "true bird of that bloody nest," [1] and that this feeling was reciprocal. Other evidence could be given, if it were necessary, to show that the influence of Buchanan ended with the ascendancy of d'Aubigny in the King's thirteenth year.

The remarks of Melville, favorable to Buchanan as they are, indicate that the King's second tutor, Peter Young, adopted a more tactful and possibly a wiser attitude. When he returned from Geneva to enter upon his duties, he was a young man of about twenty-five. Buchanan speaks of him as "adolescens probus et doctus"; [2] and the testimony of the English representative Bowes, who in 1580 wrote that he would take no money for his influence over the King, [3] is in itself, considering the practices of the period, an ample certificate of character. Young was appointed Master Almoner (October 25, 1577), Envoy to Denmark (1585 and later), one of the "Octavians" in charge of the King's finances (1596), and tutor to Prince Charles and "chief overseer" of his household (1604). [4] To him fell perhaps the larger share of the King's instruction and entertainment in his boyhood.

Neither of the tutors could refrain from the temptation to turn his apt pupil into a prodigy of learning. He was "the sweitest sight in Europe that day," writes the diarist Melville, with an enthusiasm which cooled as the prodigy grew older, "for strange and extraordinar gifts of ingyne, judgement, memorie and language. I hard him discours, walking upe and doun in the auld Lady Marr's hand, of knawlage and ignorance, to my greit mervell and estonishment." [5] Killigrew, in another well-known passage written

---

[1] Quoted from a remark attributed to Buchanan in D. Irving, *Memoirs of the Life and Works of George Buchanan*, London, 1807, p. 169.

[2] *Opera*, ed. 1715, Vol. II; *Epistolæ*, p. 12.

[3] *Bowes' Correspondence*, Surtees Soc., p. 28, June 3, 1580.

[4] G. F. Warner, *The Library of James VI*, Scot. Hist. Soc., pp. xiii–xv.

[5] *Diary*, Bann. Club, p. 38 (1574).

just after the King's eighth birthday, wonders at his skill in translating any chapter of the Bible out of Latin into French, and out of French into English. He also danced for the envoy, and showed himself "sure a prince of great hope, if God send him life." [1] "They gar me speik Latin ar I could speik Scotis," [2] said James, with a touch of the humor and good sense he could display occasionally; but the effect of the drill is shown by the fact that in later life he could speak "Latin and French perfectly and Italian quite well," [3] and knew a great part of the Bible by heart, so that he could refer offhand to chapter and verse. [4]

More exact information regarding the King's studies, evidently at a somewhat later period, may be gained from an undated schedule of his daily tasks, written by the tutor Young and included by Thomas Smith in his notice of Young's life. [5] "After prayers," according to this document, "a period was devoted to Greek, with reading from the New Testament, Isocrates, or Plutarch's Apothegms, and practice in Greek grammar. The rest of the forenoon was given to Livy, Justin, Cicero, or Scottish and other history, and the afternoon to exercises in composition, or, if time permitted, to the study of arithmetic, geography and astronomy, dialectic, or rhetoric." A bill of Gibson, the King's bookbinder, presented before 1580, includes in its list of books a number of school texts evidently worn with use, among them such works as Euclid's *Elementa*, the *Questiones Logicæ* and *Questiones Physicæ* of Freigius, Cardanus on the significance of eclipses, Orontius's *De Fœtu Humano*, Volphius's *De Perseverantia*, Cassiodorus's *Dialectica*, Beza's *De Notis Ecclesiæ*, and Hemmingsen's *De Superstitionibus Magicis*. [6] The King's later writings show his

---

[1] Letter to Walsingham, June 30, 1574. Quoted in Tytler's *Hist. of Scot.*, Vol. II, p. 9.

[2] *Apothegmata Regis*, in Young's MSS. Quoted by Warner, p. xiii.

[3] *Cal. S. P. Venetian*, Vol. X, No. 22 (1603).

[4] *Cal. S. P Spanish, 1586–1595*, p. 250.

[5] *Vitæ Quorundam Eruditissimorum & illustrium Virorum*, London, 1707, p. 6.

[6] Maitland Club *Miscellany*, Vol. I, p. 17. The payment of the bill is dated October 1, 1580.

training in dialectic, his wide reading in theology and the
theory of government as revealed in history, and his special
fondness for the magic, witchcraft, and pseudo-physiology
of Pliny, Plutarch, and such contemporary writers as Hemmingsen and the physician Cardanus.[1]

The library gathered together for these pursuits was
probably larger and more varied than any other in Scotland
at the time.[2] Many of Queen Mary's books were included,
about a hundred and fifty of which had been left in Edinburgh Castle and the remainder in part handed over to
James. This collection was rich in medieval romances and
in the works of contemporary French poets. The King's
own library contained over four hundred volumes, which,
with other recorded acquisitions not mentioned by Young,
bring the total to about six hundred books accessible to
the King in 1578. Buchanan and Young were guided in
their purchases by their own scholarly tastes and a solici-
tude for the edification rather than the entertainment of
their pupil. More than half of the books in Young's list
are, as one might expect, in Latin, perhaps one hundred and
fifty in French, a few in Greek, Italian, and Spanish, and
scarcely two score in English. The latter include Ascham's
Toxophilus and *The Schoolmaster*, Elyot's *Governour* and
The Institution of a Gentleman, Hoby's translation of *Il
Cortegiano*, and almost nothing else of literary interest —
though Gibson's list ends pleasantly with *Lustie Juventus*.
In contrast with the absence of English verse, James had
in French, either in his own collection or his mother's, the
poems of Ronsard nearly complete, Du Bellay's *Æneid* and
L'Olive augmentée, and volumes of Marot, Magny, Thyard,

[1] Cf. notes, especially to poems XVII, XVIII, LIV, and LVI.

[2] Lists of the books left by Mary at Holyrood and Edinburgh Castle were
published by the Bannatyne Club in the *Inventaires de la Royne Descosse*, 1863,
and carefully annotated in Julian Sharman's monograph, *The Library of Mary
Queen of Scots*, London, 1889. The Edinburgh Castle list, together with
Gibson's bill and an earlier bill for thirty-one books purchased for James, had
previously been printed in the Maitland Club *Miscellany* cited above. The
King's books are given in G. F. Warner's *Library of James VI, 1573–1583*,
Scot. Hist. Soc., 1893, from a MS. in the hand of Peter Young, with intro-
duction and notes, to which the reader is referred for more detailed study.

and Du Bartas; in Italian, Dante and Petrarch; and the classics in abundance both in the original and in translation. One of the most interesting portions of Young's MS. is a list, later than the rest, of forty-six books taken from Stirling to Holyrood House, November 11, 1583, presumably chosen by the King himself, who was then in his eighteenth year, and at a time coincident with his first essays in verse under Montgomerie.[1] Aside from a dozen or more volumes of the classics, and political treatises such as Cheke's *Hurt of Sedition*, *The True Religion and Popery*, and Buchanan's *De Jure Regni*, the list includes Daneau's *Geographica Poetica*, Ronsard's *La Françiade* and two volumes of his *Poémes*,[2] and Du Bellay's *Musagnœmachie* and *L'Olive augmentée*. The latter items may indicate the King's preparatory reading for the sonnets and the treatise on the art of poesy in *The Essayes of a Prentise*. Aside from the influence of older native poetry, the poetic theory and practice of both James and Montgomerie were based chiefly on French models.

Nothing very serious, one might think, could be wrong with a young gentleman who would undertake so profitable a course of reading as the one just outlined. James, indeed, emerged or escaped from the hands of his guardians a mixture of curious and not wholly unlikable qualities. Whatever he was willing to pretend or call himself for political purposes, it must be admitted that his religious convictions were reasonably founded and sincere. From the worst vices of his family and nation he was free; he did not drink to excess, and he was so continent that he excited the anxiety of the court; and he was reasonably observant of the rest of the commandments, if one excepts the third, fourth,

---

[1] Warner, pp. xxvii, xxxv. That the King selected the books may be surmised chiefly from the fact that they were in line with his activities in the following winter.

[2] In the 1567 edition of Ronsard the third volume, entitled *Poêmes*, contained his *Abrégé de l'Art Poétique françois*. The books James took were in quarto, and this was the only edition of Ronsard of that size. Both this treatise and Du Bellay's *Défense et Illustration de la Langue française* were among the books of Mary.

fifth, and perhaps the ninth. It should be remembered that James's middle course in politics and religion exposed him to the attack of both extremes, and especially to the abuse of writers such as Wilson, Osborne, and Welden, who, like Prynne, fed the ears of credulous Puritans with the dregs of court scandal. Curiosity hunters in the eighteenth century and later found the accounts of these "caper-witted" writers, as Bishop Hackett calls them, more attractive reading than those of soberer annalists, and even the James of *The Fortunes of Nigel*, vivid as it is, is an effective caricature and not a truthful portrait. Its influence, however, is not easily counteracted by the soberer judgments of Von Ranke, Gardiner, Pattison, Spedding, Tytler, and the majority of later historians. Most of the King's faults can be traced to love of pleasure and lack of self-control, which were inherited traits; his lavishness of expense, devotion to favorites, dislike of business, impatience at prolonged mental exertion or even tedious entertainment, — all are manifestations of common Stuart failings. Though he had the intelligence and wit of his family, he had no great share of its dignity. His fits of tears, his absurd displays of affection, his coarseness, — though this is not in his writings and perhaps did not so much trouble old courtiers of Elizabeth like Sir John Harington,[1] — made it hard for him to command the respect even of his friends.

---

[1] Author of *The Metamorphosis of Ajax* (1596). His *Nugæ Antiquæ* (ed. Th. Park, 1804) is one of the chief sources for court gossip of the first ten years of James's reign in England. Portions of it, however, should be taken in the light of his earlier performance.

II

THE STUDY OF POETRY UNDER MONT-GOMERIE

"Beloved Sanders maistre of our art."
— *Admonition*, l. 2.

The arrival in Scotland of Esmé Stuart d'Aubigny in September, 1579,[1] and the King's "first and magnificent" entry into Edinburgh in the next month, mark the beginning of a complete change from the latter's quiet life at Stirling. D'Aubigny was a cousin of James's father, a man of "cumlie proportion and civil behaviour," according to Melville, "upright, just, and gentle, but wanting experience in the state of the country."[2] "False"[3] has been added; yet it is likely that his influence over the young King was gained at first by nothing more objectionable than his personal charm and the boy's natural feeling for his kindred. Together, amid the grief and railings of the Kirk, they set about the overthrow of the Regent Morton and the collection at court of more congenial followers. "Papists with great ruffes and syde bellies were suffered in the presence of the Kynge."[4] "His Majesties chaste ears were frequently abused with unknown Italian and French forms of oaths, days were turned into nights, and Arran's mistress infected the air of the court." In milder language, James was easily distracted by less elevated phases of humanism than the study of the classics and Calvinistic theology.

Among those who found the change not unpleasant was

---

[1] D'Aubigny arrived at Stirling September 15. James entered Edinburgh on the 29th of the same month, but the formal celebration did not take place until the 15th of October. (*Moysie's Memoirs*, Bann. Club, p. 25.)

[2] *Memoirs*, Bann. Club, p. 240.

[3] Andrew Lang, *History of Scotland*, Vol. II, p. 264. D'Aubigny is thought to have served the Catholic interest (which, be it said in his favor, was by no means his own) throughout his stay in Scotland.

[4] *Bowes' Correspondence*, Surtees Soc., p. 136.

Alexander Montgomerie, author of *The Cherrie and the Slae*, and the only Scottish poet of importance who was writing in this period. In the next ten years his life connects itself closely with the King's, and affords the best approach to the latter's relations with Scottish literature. There is reason to suppose that he numbered among his companions the English poet Constable; he was the leader of the quasi-literary group of envoys and intelligencers who were about the court and hailed in sonnets the issues of the King's poems; and, as will appear later, he was the King's guide in his first ventures into verse and criticism.

The date of his birth is still uncertain, but the recently published researches of Mr. George Stevenson[1] make it clear that, while he was born not later than 1545, he belonged to a younger generation of the Hessilheid Montgomeries than the one with which he has hitherto been connected, and that his mother, who died after a long widowhood in 1583, was a great granddaughter of Sir John Stewart of Dernely, first Earl of Lennox, from whom James and d'Aubigny were also directly descended. The poet was thus a member of the Stewart clan, and his kinship with the King helps to explain the favor in which he stood at court. Of his early life little is known, but there is reason to believe that he was in the Low Countries at some time during the seventies,[2] and afterward about the court as a follower of

---

[1] *Poems of Alexander Montgomerie, Supplementary Volume*, Scottish Text Society, 1910.

[2] Cf. l. 591 of *Polwart and Montgomeries Flyting:* —
    "Syne forward to Flanders fast fled or he ceast."
A Captain Robert Montgomerie — whose friendship with the Hessilheid branch of the family is shown by the fact that his name appears, with the title added, as prolocutor for Hugh of Hessilheid in a lawsuit (Pitcairn's *Crim. Trials*, Vol. I, p. 62) — was sent to Flanders in the spring of 1573 with a force of about three thousand horse and foot (*Cal. S. P. For., 1572–1574*, Nos. 460, 1114, 1163). The poet may have accompanied this expedition. Young, in his list of the King's books (Warner, pp. l, lix), written before 1578, records two gifts, one "Gottin fra Capten Montgomery," and the other "Donnée par le Capitaine Robert Montgommery." The difference in the form of the entries may serve to distinguish between the two captains, and the gifts of books would indicate their return from abroad. Robert Hackett came back from Flanders the next year with at least a dozen (*ibid.*, p. xxxix).

Morton.[1] The only poems of his which belong clearly in this period are *The Navigatioun* and *The Cartell of the Thre Ventrous Knichts*, written for the King's first entry into Edinburgh.

That the poet joined the Lennox faction at court, and during the next ten years was first a "familiar servitour" and afterward a pensioner of the King, is established by evidence drawn both from his writings and from documents of the period. On March 5, 1579–1580, d'Aubigny was made Earl of Lennox, and soon after acquired the large revenues of the Bishopric of Glasgow. Robert Montgomerie, a kinsman of the poet,[2] was appointed "tulchan" archbishop, as the means by which the money might reach Lennox. He was thus a follower of Lennox as early as 1581, and this bears out the evidence in a sonnet of Montgomerie (XVII, in the numbering of Cranstoun's edition for the Scottish Text Society) that the poet was in the same service and in this way a member of the royal household. For later reference the sonnet is given in full; the "suete Duke" was Lennox's son Ludovic, who at the time when the poem was written was about nineteen years old,[3] and the "umquhyle Maister" was not Morton, as has generally been supposed, but Lennox himself. This is shown by the fact that Henry Keir, one of the companions mentioned, was Lennox's private secretary [4] and a great practicer against

---

[1] This may be gathered from a reference in Melville's *Diary* (p. 45, *c.* 1576) to a "Capten Mongummerie, a guid honest man, the Regent's domestic." The given name is omitted, but the term "domestic" and the joke in the context suggest the poet. Cf. XXII, note.

[2] It has been supposed that he was the poet's brother, but for this Stevenson finds no documentary evidence. He was appointed minister in Stirling in 1572, at the request of Morton (*Acts of Gen. Ass. of the Kirk*, p. 135). On his acceptance of the bishopric, he was excommunicated by the Kirk, and on one occasion attacked by an Edinburgh mob with stones and rotten eggs, an episode the account of which so amused the King that he lay down by the Inch of Perth unable to contain himself for laughter. According to James, he was a "seditious loon"; the Kirk accused him of opposing the "doctrine of Christ, who pronounceth that the most part are rebellious, and perish," and related that he had been found drunk and in pursuit of his servant with a drawn whinger (Calderwood, *Hist. of the Kirk*, Vol. VI, pp. 580, 635).

[3] *Historie of King James Sext*, Bann. Club, p. 189.

[4] *Cal. S. P. For.,* January 15, 1580.

the Kirk.[1] Constable was either Archibald Douglas, the Scottish representative in London, who occupied the curious position of an envoy paid by the government to which he was sent, and who was sometimes referred to by this title;[2] or Henry Constable, the English sonneteer and Catholic emissary, whose activities make his intimacy with Keir and Montgomerie at least equally probable.[3]

[To his Majestie, for his pension.]

Adeu, my King, court, cuntrey, and my kin;
Adeu, suete Duke, vhose father held me deir;
Adeu, companiones, Constable and Keir:
Thrie treuar hairts, I trou, shall neuer tuin.
If byganes to revolve I suld begin,
  My tragedie wald cost you mony a teir
  To heir hou hardly I am handlit heir,
  Considring once the honour I wes in.
Shirs, ye haif sene me griter with his Grace,
  And with your umquhyle Maister, to, and myne;
Quha thogt the Poet somtyme worth his place,
  Suppose ye sie they shot him out sensyne.
Sen wryt, nor wax, nor word is not a word;
I must perforce ga seik my fathers suord.

By the Raid of Ruthven, August 22, 1582, the opponents of Lennox secured possession of the King's person and drove the Duke back to France, where he died in May of the next year. Montgomerie, however, remained in the household, for, on April 24, 1583, he appeared as the King's messenger before the General Assembly of the Kirk, forbidding them to remove the principal or members of the University of Glasgow.[4] Again in Calderwood, in August

---

  [1] Melville's *Memoirs*, p. 240. In August, 1585, Sir Edward Stafford wrote from Paris that "John [Henry?] Keyer, a Scot, sometime secretary of the Duke of Lennox, had been with the Queen of Scots in disguise" (*Cal. S. P. Sco.*, p. 440).
  [2] Calderwood, Vol. VI, p. 486.
  [3] Cf. p. xxxvii.
  [4] Calderwood, *History of the Kirk*, Vol. III, p. 708.

of the same year, we learn that "the King's old household
servants were changid for the most part, and the rest were
likewise to be removed, as James Murray of Powmaes,
Captain Montgomerie, etc." [1] This change it is difficult to
explain, unless it was a concession to the demands of the
Kirk following James's escape in June from the control
of the Ruthven nobles. But it is quite unlikely that it
represents any withdrawal of favor; Montgomerie was
now placed on a pension of five hundred merks a year,
granted by James, July 7, 1583, and paid regularly until
1586, when the poet left Scotland on an errand abroad for
the King.[2]

In November of 1583 the interesting packet of political
tracts and French verse was brought from Stirling to Holyrood,[3] and in the ensuing winter James seems to have
settled down to the examination of Scottish histories, the
censorship of treasonable documents, and the study and
composition of poetry. The *Phœnix*, lamenting the death
of Lennox and referring to the arrival of his son,[4] was written
at this time, and is the longest and best of the poems which
appeared the next year in *The Essayes of a Prentise*.[5] The
translation from Du Bartas in the *Essayes* may belong to
the same period, but the boyish crudity of the *Reulis and
cautelis* and the twelve "sonnets and suites to the gods"
suggests that they were composed still earlier. The "Song,
the first verses that ever the King made" (LIII), was written, according to the heading in Calderwood, when he was
"fyfteene yeere old," and there is other evidence that his

[1] *Ibid.*, Vol. VIII, App., p. 250. Since Montgomerie appears as a "sirvi-
tour of the Kingis Majestie" in a document dated December 30, 1584 (Stevenson, p. 304), it is reasonable to conclude that these earlier references are to
him.
[2] Cf. the grant authorizing the restoration of his pension, *Reg. of the Privy
Seal of Scotland*, March 21, 1588–1589.
[3] Cf. p. xxiii. · Buchanan's *De Jure Regni*, which was in the packet, and
his *History* were condemned by act of Parliament the next year (*Acts of the
Parliaments of Scotland*, Vol. III, p. 296).
[4] Ludovic landed at Leith, November 13, 1583.
[5] There seem to have been two issues of this volume; some copies bear
the date 1584 and others 1585.

poetical experiments began as early as 1581.[1] Whatever
the exact date, it is clear that they were carried on under the
guidance of Montgomerie and not of Buchanan, who died
September 29, 1582, and some time before had ceased to
perform his duties as tutor. The King's reliance on the
master poet is everywhere traceable in both his precepts
and his practice.

To this period may also be assigned Montgomerie's
Flyting with Polwart, the King's enjoyment of which is
spoken of in one of Montgomerie's sonnets (XXVII): —

> "Vhose Highnes laughed som tym for to look
> Hou I chaist Polwart from the chimney nook."

The *Flyting* is true to its uncomely type, and to modern
taste more grotesquely coarse than either lascivious or
amusing; but it is not necessary to make it the chief index
of James's early taste in poetry — he was also the translator of Du Bartas's *Uranie, ou Muse Celeste*.

Montgomerie's poem, like the King's *Admonition* (LI),
illustrates the good-natured fellowship which existed between the young monarch and his poetical familiars. Cele-
brations inspired by Bacchus as well as the Muses were not
infrequent. Indeed, from such evidence as we can gather
— the joke on Archbishop Adamson,[2] the boisterous tone
of the *Flyting* and similar pieces, his final surrender to the
god of wine [3] — one pictures "beloved Sanders" as a jovial,
not altogether reputable character such as Scott would have
enjoyed painting, gifted with intelligence and some genius,
yet quite capable of the rôle of court jester or abbot of un-
reason when occasion permitted.

The order of March 21, 1588–1589, restoring Montgomerie's pension,[4] informs us that he left Scotland on the
King's business in the autumn of 1586, with license to "pass
of this realme to the pairtis of France, Flanders, Spaine,

---

[1] Stevenson places the *Flyting* in 1582, and suggests that the King's *Admonition* was written not long after.

[2] Cf. XXII, note.   [3] Cf. XXXIV, XLV, and notes.   [4] Cf. p. xxix, note.

and otheris beyond sey . . . quheras he remanit continew-
allie sensyne, detaynit and halden in prison." His destina-
tion and the nature of his errand have remained unknown,
though the time, just preceding the execution of Mary,
his intimacy with Constable and Keir, and references in his
sonnets to Archbishop Beaton, Mary's representative in
Paris, show that he was associated with members of the
Catholic party. A hitherto unnoted letter from T. Fowler
to Archibald Douglas in London, November 25, 1588,[1]
makes it likely that his imprisonment was in England. The
given name is again omitted, but the date and the circumstances of the detention at once connect the reference
with the poet. Fowler's statement that Montgomerie was
"unacquainted with trouble" may be taken with many
allowances.

During his absence, his pension was stopped, and a number of his sonnets (XIV–XXX)[2] deal with his efforts by
legal proceedings and direct appeal to the King to have it
restored. Since they were all written during a short period
and for a special purpose, one can hardly draw a general
conclusion regarding the author's petulant melancholy of
temperament or undignified servility. His "real and sincere" passion for Lady Margaret Montgomerie, to whom
he addressed sonnets at the time of her marriage in 1582,

---

[1] *Cal. Hatfield MSS.*, Pt. III, p. 374. Fowler complains of the seizure of
his papers by the English authorities: "Always if they would deliver my
house and stuff, I shall be glad, and more of Montgomery's release, which I
beseech you to procure as much as you may, for he is honest and not ac-
quainted with trouble, and what they have to say to him God knows. I
wot not, but I would gladly know whereupon they examined him, and what
he hath done with my books." Fowler was an Englishman resident in
Edinburgh and connected with the Lennox family. He was executor of
the Countess of Lennox's will, and was intrusted by Queen Mary with jewels
intended for Lady Arabella Stuart. These got into the hands of James;
hence, perhaps, the seizure of Fowler's papers.

[2] The mention in one of these sonnets (XXV) of the poets Alexander Scott
and Robert Semple shows that they were still alive in 1588. But Scott, the
references to whom as a burgess of Edinburgh are pointed out by T. F. Henderson (*Scottish Vernacular Lit.*, p. 241), was perhaps also the burgess of that
name mentioned in *Cal. S. P. Sco.*, July 20, 1591, who had sent letters of
complaint to England regarding the debts of an English agent in Edinburgh

is also wholly mythical, since she was many years his junior and of a higher social station. In spite of the restoration, his pension was still withheld, and it is doubtful if Montgomerie ever regained favor at court. James was in Denmark from October, 1589, until May of the next year, and after his return there was another reordering and reduction of his household.

The King's *Epitaphe* (XXXIV) and a second sonnet referring to Montgomerie (XLV) may conveniently be considered at this point, since they make it highly probable that the poet's death occurred before the King's departure for England. After 1603, James wrote little verse, and could hardly have spoken of the Scottish writer as "our maistre poëte" and "the Prince of Poets of our land." In the *Bodleian MS.*, XLV occurs on one side of a folio which contains an early paraphrase of one of the psalms.[1] The thirteenth line of the *Epitaphe*, —

"Though to his buriall was refused the bell,"

— shows that at the time of his death Montgomerie was not in the good graces of the clergy. The latest of other trustworthy references to the poet is a denunciation, July 14, 1597, of "Alexander Montgomerie, brother to the laird of Heslott," for "arte, parte" in Hugh Barclay of Ladyland's treasonable attempt to seize Ailsa Craig as a station for Spanish troops and refuge for Catholics.[2] It is perhaps significant as a clue to the date of his death that the two earliest editions of *The Cherrie and the Slae* appeared in this year, from different MSS., but neither with any announcement, preface, or complimentary verses such as one would expect with the work of a living writer. The second, it is true, was "Prented according to a Copie corrected by the Author himselfe"; but this may refer to the MS., and, according to Mr. Stevenson,[3] the edition contains errors which make it hard to believe that it was corrected by the author. In

---

[1] *Lusus Regius*, p. 54.
[2] *Register of the Privy Council of Scotland* (cf. Stevenson, p. 334).
[3] *Poems of Alexander Montgomerie*, p. xvii.

1615, a third edition (now lost) appeared, in which the poem was increased from 930 to 1596 lines. Since it is generally admitted that this edition came out after the poet's death, there is no difficulty in assuming the enlargement to have been made prior to 1603, or even, for that matter, prior to 1597.

III

OTHER POETS IN THE SCOTTISH COURT,
1584–1603

"Quique poetas claros sodales suos vulgo vocari voluit."
— DEMPSTER.

The publication of *The Essayes of a Prentise* in 1584 was followed, it would seem, by some slackening of the King's interest in poetry.   In the winter of 1587 he was occupied "in commenting of the Apocalypse and in setting out of sermontes thereupon against the Papistes and Spainyards," though, as Melville adds, "by a piece of grait oversight, the Papists practised never mair busselie in this land. . . ."[1] In the commentary, or *Paraphrase upon the Revelation*,[2] the author by a scarcely prosaic flight of fancy connects the Pope with Anti-Christ and Catholicism with St. John's vision of the beast with seven heads and ten horns.   *Ane Fruitfull Meditatioun* on Revelation xx. 7–10 appeared in 1588, and *Ane Meditatioun* on 1 Chronicles xv. 25–29 in 1589.[3]

These pursuits were pleasantly interrupted, however, by the arrival, in May, 1587,[4] of the French poet Du Bartas, whom the King in a letter of extravagant flattery had invited to Scotland for the summer.   Du Bartas's popularity among devout Protestants was due primarily to the highly commendable character of his subject-matter, drawn as it was so largely from the Bible, —

[1] *Diary*, p. 174.
[2] 1616 Folio, pp. 1–79.
[3] For full titles, dates, etc., cf. Dickson and Edmond, *Annals of Scottish Printing*, Cambridge, 1890.
[4] Du Bartas was in London, May 7, and arrived in Scotland about the 25th (*Cal. Hatfield MSS.*, Pt. III, pp. 253, 260).

"That is a horne of plenty well repleat :
That is a storehouse riche, a learning seat,
An Ocean hudge, both lacking shore and ground,
Of heauenly eloquence a spring profound.

Let not your art so rare then be defylde,
In singing Venus, and her fethered chylde." [1]

But his fame must have been greatly increased by the
influence of James, who was one of his earliest admirers in
Scotland or England. The first portion of his masterpiece,
La Semaine, ou Creation du Monde (Paris, 1579), was presented to James by his former nurse within a year or two
of its issue,[2] and in 1584 we find him discussing the possibility of an adequate translation. The following passage
is from the *Epistle Dedicatorie* of Thomas Hudson's translation of *Judith*: [3] —

"As your Maiestie, Sir, after your accustomed and vertuous manner was sometime discoursing at Table with such
your Domestiques as chaunced to be attendants ; It pleased
your Highnesse not only to esteeme the peerless stile of the
Greeke Homer, and the Latin Virgil to be inimitable to us
(whose tongue is barbarous and corrupted) : But also to
alledge (partly throu delite your Majesty tooke in the
Hautie stile of those most famous Writers, and partly to
sounde the opinion of others) that also the loftie Phrase,
the grave inditement, the facound termes of the French
Salust (for the like resemblance) could not be followed, nor
sufficiently expressed in our rude and unpolished english
language, . . . whereupon, it pleased your Maiestie (among
the rest of his workes) to assign me, The Historie of Judith,
as an agreeable Subject to your Highnesse, to be turned by
me into English verse."
During his stay in Scotland, Du Bartas and the King

---

[1] James's translation of *L'Uranie, ou Muse Celeste* of Du Bartas, ll. 116–130
(*Essayes of a Prentise*).

[2] Warner, *Library of James VI*, p. xliii.

[3] Hudson's translation was published at Edinburgh in 1584. It is included
also in the 1608 and later editions of Sylvester.

visited the University of St. Andrews, where James had the temerity to request a lecture from the Principal, Andrew Melville — the minister who later twitched his sovereign by the arm and reminded him that he as only "God's silliew vassal." Melville spoke offhand "of the right government of Chryst, and in effect refuted the haill Actes of Parliament maid against the discipline thairof, to the grait instruction of his auditor, except the king allean, who was verie angrie all that night." The next day he had so far recovered as to partake of "a bankett of wett and dry confections. . . . wherat His Maiestie camped verie merrelie a guid whyll." [1] On his guest's departure in September, James gave him "a chaine of 1000 crowns, made him knight, and accompanied him to the sea side, where he made him promise to return again." [2] The French poet repaid these honors by a translation of the King's *Lepanto*, with a fulsome preface and dedicatory sonnet. This is printed with the original and the King's translation of Du Bartas's *Furies* in the *Exercises at vacant houres*.[3]

Two years later, a second political visitor arrived in Scotland, just at the time when the King, alone at Craigmillar Castle, was eagerly awaiting the arrival of his bride from Denmark, and easing his restless mind by penning songs and sonnets.[4] This was the English poet Henry Constable, whose appearance in Scotland at this time is indicated by evidence both in his own poems and in contemporary documents. On October 20, 1589, T. Fowler wrote Burleigh that "Roger Dalton [Aston?] is exceeding great with young Constable and hath brought him to secret conference sundry times with Victor [James]. He hath commission from Ernestus [Essex] and from Rialta and Richardo [Lady and Lord Riche]." [5] His errand in Scotland, as the letter states, was to secure the King's friend-

---

[1] J. Melville's *Diary*, p. 170.

[2] *Extracts from the Despatches of M. Courcelles*, Bann. Club, p. 80.

[3] Printed also as a separate leaflet of 14 pages, *La Lepanthe de Jaques I*, Walde-grave, Edinburgh, 1591.

[4] Cf. note on the *Amatoria*, pp. 69–71.

[5] *Cal. Hatfield MSS.*, Pt. III, p. 438.

ship for Lady Arabella Stuart, and no doubt had some connection also with the royal marriage, which had been arranged for September 29, and for which a masque and masquers had been sent to Scotland by Elizabeth.[1] It may be remembered that, from 1584 on, Constable was an active Catholic messenger both at home and abroad. By November 2, he was back again in London, where he was addressed by Robert Douglas in a friendly letter of that date from Edinburgh referring to the King's regard for him and to a manuscript of his poems.[2]

Among Constable's sonnets are a series of four addressed to James, — the first "to the King of Scots, whome as yet he has not seen," the second "touching the subject of his poems, dedicated wholie to heavenly matters," the third "upon occasion of a Sonnet the King wrote in complaint of a contrarie [wind] which hindred the arrivall of the Queene out of Denmark," and the fourth "upon occasion of his long stay in Denmark, by reason of the coldnesse of the winter, and freezing of the sea."[3] The dates of these compositions are fixed by the fact that the news of the storm and Anne's delay reached Scotland September 15, 1589, and the king left on October 22, to seek his betrothed in person.

If the Constable mentioned in Montgomerie's sonnet (p. xxviii) was the poet, one may suppose the meeting of the two writers to have taken place at this time, or perhaps earlier during Montgomerie's stay in London. The possibility of their friendship is increased by the fact that Constable's sonnet beginning, —

"Thine eye, the glasse where I behold my heart,"

appears in slightly altered form among the Drummond MS. poems of Montgomerie.[4]

[1] Collier, *Annals of the Stage*, Vol. I, p. 290.

[2] *Cal. Hatfield MSS.*, Pt. III, p. 442.

[3] *Diana: Sonnets and other Poems of Henry Constable*, ed. W. C. Hazlitt, London, 1859, pp. 33-35.

[4] The original authorship of the sonnet must be conceded to Constable, since it is an integral part of the series of nine "arguments" of seven sonnets

Constable's later visits to Scotland are more fully re-corded in the state papers of the period, and have in part been noted by his biographers. In December, 1595, the Earl of Errol gave a book to the King, at which the King was offended, and which Quin, an Irish poet in the court, ascribed to Constable.[1] Colville refers to it as a seditious book in favor of Spain. In March, 1599, Constable himself arrived in Scotland and offered his services to the King, but was refused an audience and forced to account for himself before the Lords of the Session.[2] Later he is described as an agent of the Pope accompanying the Lord of Boniton, and on September 22 about to return to France.[3] In April, 1600, he sent the King news from Aragon, apparently as his paid correspondent, and in July of the same year a book which he had written, but which at this late date could hardly have been, as Mr. Sidney Lee infers,[4] a copy of Diana. After the death of Elizabeth he ventured to return from the Continent to England, and April 28, 1604, was "a few days ago imprisoned" for writing to the Papal Nuncio in France stating that "the King had no religion at all and that everything he did was governed by political expediency."[5] In August following, the Venetian Secretary wrote that Constable had been released from the Tower and confined to his own house.[6] Little is known of his career from this time until his death abroad in 1613.

Both Constable and Montgomerie contributed laudatory sonnets to the first editions of the King's poems, the former to the *Exercises at vacant houres* of 1591, and the latter to the *Essayes of a Prentise*. Other more or less literary figures who enjoyed the King's favor were permitted similar dis-

each into which the *Diana* sequence is divided, and since it occurs in the Todd MS. of 1590 and among the twenty-three sonnets of the first edition of 1592. Montgomerie's version is a re-working of Constable's in the Scottish dialect, with the object, perhaps, as Brotanek suggests, of avoiding the rhyme-in-terms (come-become) which the *Reulis and cautelis* condemns, and which occurs but once in Montgomerie's poems. Cf. Brotanek's study of Montgomerie, *Wiener Beiträge*, Vol. III.

[1] *Cal. S. P. Sco.*, p. 702. [4] *Dict. Nat. Biog.*, under Constable.
[2] *Ibid.*, pp. 773, 776. [5] *Cal. S. P. Venetian, 1603–1605*, No. 213.
[3] *Ibid.*, pp. 781, 784. [6] *Ibid.*, No. 250.

tinction. Their names are indicated in the *Essayes* by the
subscribed initials T. H., R. H., M. W., M. W. F., and A. M.,
which have been identified, the first two with the brothers
Thomas and Robert Hudson, the fourth with Master
William Fowler, and the last with Montgomerie. The
third initials, M. W., may indicate Master William (Fowler),
or possibly, by transposition, William Murray, one of
the King's four valets of the chamber, whom Montgomerie
addresses as "belovit brother"[1] in a friendly sonnet from
London. The poems of 1591 are greeted by Fowler, Constable, and Henry Lok (or Locke), and in Greek and Latin
verses by Hadrian Damman. Locke and Constable were
Englishmen, the one of Puritan sympathies and the other
a Catholic, and Damman was a native of Flanders.

The lives of these gentlemen are less worthy of note for
their own sake than as an indication of the King's literary
intercourse and the culture of his Scottish court. The
Hudsons belonged to a family of four brothers, of English
descent,[2] who were musicians to the King in his earliest
childhood. They are mentioned in the first *Establishment
of the Household*,[3] in March, 1567, as "Violaris: Mekill
Thomas Hudsoun, Robert Hudsoun, James Hudsoun,[4]
William Hudsoun"; and in the reorganized household of
1591 they hold the same offices, with the privilege of a
table to themselves at meals.[5] Thomas was appointed
Master of the Chapel Royal, June 5, 1586, and was continued in the position by acts of Parliament in 1587 and
again in 1592.[6] In Allott's *England's Parnassus* (1600), he

---

[1] Sonnet LXV, S. T. S. edition. Cf. also James's "William Mow," LI, 112, and note.

[2] For evidence of their nationality, cf. XXVI, 4, and note.

[3] G. Chalmers, *Life of Mary Queen of Scots*, Philadelphia, 1822, p. 135.

[4] James Hudson was recommended to Elizabeth by the King in a letter dated April 24, 1583 (*S. P. Sco.*), and from this time on was employed as an agent and correspondent either of James or Cecil. The Venetian Secretary speaks of him as the King's "Envoy in Ordinary" in London. (*S. P. Ven.*, April 24, 1603). He was afterward appointed a groom of the chamber with a pension of £120 (Record Office, Docquets, April 1, 1604).

[5] *Papers relative to the Marriage of King James*, Bann. Club, App. II, p. 33.

[6] *Acts of the Parliaments of Scotland*, Vol. III, pp. 489, 563.

was honored, together with his royal master, by a surprisingly large number of selections, forty-seven in all and amounting to 392 lines, taken from his translation of *Judith*. He is also included, with the King and Locke, in the list of forty or more contributors to Bodenham's *Belvedére, or The Garden of the Muses*, published in the same year. The first of these collections contains some distinguished verse, but Hudson's, it must be admitted, is of a type to warrant the disparaging remarks about "crows and kestrels" in *The Return from Parnassus* of 1602. In this satire, both he and Locke are advised to sleep quiet "among the shavings of the press, and let your books lie in some old nooks among old boots and shoes, so you may avoid my censure."[1] The verse of his which has survived consists of an epitaph on Sir Richard Maitland[2] (d. 1586), prefatory sonnets for James's poems and for Fowler's *Triumphs of Petrarch*, and *The History of Judith*,[3] translated from Du Bartas and published in Edinburgh, 1584. Robert Hudson wrote sonnets on the same themes as his brother, and is addressed by Montgomerie in a series of four sonnets (XXV–XXIX) which are really a single poem seeking his assistance at court.

Fowler's *Triumphs of Petrarch*, just mentioned, was written, like Hudson's *Judith*, at the request of the King, and is preserved in manuscript, with a sonnet sequence entitled *The Tarantula of Love*, in the Edinburgh University Library.[4] The title "P. of Hawicke," which is given Fowler in the MS., is explained by an entry in the *Records of the Burgh of Edinburgh*, May 29, 1589, to the effect that "William Fowler, persoun of Hawick" had been appointed

---

[1] Temple Dramatists edition, London, 1905, I, ii, ll. 56, 147–155. The editor follows W. C. Hazlitt in describing Locke and Hudson as "satirists of the time . . . the Bavius and Mævius of that age." They were *poetæ minimi*, but not satirists.

[2] This, with Robert's epitaph and other sonnets probably of the same authorship, is in Pinkerton's *Ancient Scottish Poems*, Vol. II, p. 350 ff.

[3] "At your owne commandement enterprised, corrected by your Maiest. owne hande, and dedicated to your owne Highnesse." — *Epistle dedicatorie*.

[4] For a description of the MS., cf. XXIX, note.

by the Council to accompany the Ambassador Peter Young to Denmark — perhaps to discover the true religion of the Princess Anne, or to watch the expenditure of the ten thousand pounds borrowed from the city for the journey. The term *parson* is used in contemporary documents to indicate a layman appointed to a religious benefice; and since Fowler's name does not occur elsewhere in church records, it is to be supposed that he held the living merely for its revenue.

A William Fowler, who may have been either the poet or a son of Thomas Fowler,[1] acted as an agent of Walsingham's in 1582 and 1583, and in this capacity accompanied the Duke of Lennox (d'Aubigny) on his departure from Scotland. In a letter of Fowler's, d'Aubigny is quoted as saying that "your mother's house was the first I entered, on coming to Scotland, and the last I quitted on leaving the country."[2] This statement is explained, perhaps, by the fact that a Fowler is mentioned as a servant of the Lennox family as early as 1565, and by evidence that their house in Edinburgh was sometimes used for banquets[3] or for the entertainment of noble guests. William later became secretary to Queen Anne, and as assistant to Sir Patrick Lesley was chief contriver of the celebration at Prince Henry's baptism [4] (July 16, 1594), an account of which he afterward published. He went to England in the Queen's service, and held his secretaryship until 1612, when he was succeeded by Sir Robert Aytoun.[5] The mother of William Drummond of Hawthornden was Fowler's sister, and his father was also of the court as one of the King's gentlemen ushers.[6] In Scotland, and later in England, the young poet must have

---

[1] Cf. p. xxxi, note.

[2] Tytler, *History of Scotland*, ed. 1866, Vol. VIII, p. 127.

[3] *Cal. S. P. Sco.*, May 22, 1589.

[4] *Letters of Colville*, Bann. Club, p. 112. For reference to the description of the ceremonies, cf. LIV, 48, note.

[5] Cf. p. lxxiv. According to Masson (*William Drummond of Hawthornden*, London, 1873, p. 31), Fowler died in 1614. For the attempts of Donne to secure the reversion of his office, cf. p. lxv.

[6] Nichols, *Progresses of James*, Vol. II, p. 263, inserts an order on the town of Southampton for royal guards, presented by Sir John Drummond, Gentleman Usher, August 4, 1609.

seen much of his uncle, and may have been led to the pursuit of literature by his influence. Fowler's verse,[1] together with the shorter poems of Montgomerie, came into the possession of Drummond and was preserved in his library.

Henry Locke, the last of the prefatory sonneteers, was a poet of slightly greater prominence. Bodenham, for his quotations from Locke in *Belvedére*, probably used the volume of friendly and devotional sonnets "by H. L. Gentleman"[2] which was licensed for publication in 1593, and issued again in 1597 with a number of scriptural paraphrases under the title of "Ecclesiastes, otherwise called The Preacher — Whereunto are annexed sundrie sonets of a feeling conscience of the same authors." Dr. Grosart, in his reprint of a part of this volume,[3] includes the sonnet printed in the *Exercises at vacant houres* (wrongly referred to as *The Essayes of a Prentise*) and if in his introductory biography he had followed up this clue, he might have shown that the greater part of Locke's life was spent as an envoy or political intelligencer. He was engaged in this service as early as 1581,[4] but it was not until ten years later[5] that he was sent to Scotland to help carry out Elizabeth's ingenious and persistent policy of setting Scottish lords against their king. His letters show that his activities continued intermittently until 1602. His intrigues

---

[1] Two sonnets by Fowler and a number of his letters are found in Nichols, *Progresses*, Vol. I, pp. 251, 261, etc. The verses have the headings, *Sonnet uppon a Horloge of the Clock at Sir George More's, 1603,* and *To Lady Arabella Stuart.* Fowler's letters to the Earl and Lady Shrewsbury indicate continued devotion to the Lennox family and a hand in the Lady Arabella's match-making, but not, as Disraeli (quoted by Nichols) supposes, a desire to present himself to the King's cousin as a suitor.

[2] In Bodenham's list of contributors (cf. p. lvi), Locke, Constable, and Churchyard are the only ones distinguished by the title " Esq."

[3] *Miscellanies of the Fuller Worthies' Library,* 1871, Vol. II. The article on Locke in *Dict. Nat. Biog.* is based chiefly on Grosart's introduction.

[4] *Cal. S. P. For., 1580–1581.*

[5] *Cal. Hatfield MSS.,* Pt. IV, p. 111, R. Douglas to A. Douglas, May 18, 1591 : Locke "has been in these parts . . . half a year and more . . . and his majesty and the queen have conceived no little opinion of his honest behavior, so that they would willingly employ him in their service." Cf. *Cal. S. P. Sco.,* for Locke's correspondence between May, 1591, and February, 1602.

with Bothwell and with the latter's fellow-plotter, John Colville — who nearly always addresses Locke as "beloved brother" — sufficiently explain his loss of employment after 1603, and his vain appeals to Cecil from Gatehouse and the Clink.

It is not perhaps too much to assume that the men whose lives have been outlined — at least Montgomerie, Fowler, and the Hudsons — were among the King's most intimate companions in his youth. He matured early, and was busy in statecraft and intrigue before most young noblemen of his age were free from their tutors and about the court. The nobility who surrounded him were not only older, but raw and reckless, involved in feuds among themselves and in " bands " against the crown. Scarcely one of them could be fully trusted. But the members of his household he had known from childhood, and while they were his servants and likely to treat him with deference, James was not one who let rank stand in the way of familiarity. Though *The Essayes of a Prentise* appeared without his name on the title-page, its authorship was obvious, and we should expect it to have been welcomed by a more impressive array of sonneteers, if James could have found noblemen willing to humor his literary bent or capable of penning a sonnet, and if he had not wished to give his fellow-experimenters an opportunity to see themselves in print.

Not much, to be sure, can be said for the characters of these literary friends. Most of them were capable of playing a double part and turning their friendship to profit. But they were men of culture and travel, who could bring the King in touch with England and the Continent. Several of them were envoys either of the King or of foreign powers, and the circumstance helps to explain the rapidity with which literary tendencies passed from one country to another in this period. It is clear, also, that scholarship was considered a key to royal favor. Foreign governments recognized this in their choice of representatives; such men as Du Bartas, Sir Edward and Sir Henry Wotton, Sir Robert Sidney, Constable, and Locke, all of whom visited Scotland, may well have been selected with an eye to the King's tastes. The King's Scottish favorites were men of culture. Lennox, the earliest, was a courtier of polish and address. The Maitlands, father and sons, were possessed of literary talents rare enough in the Scotland of that day. Sir James, the Chancellor, "had intellect," writes Mr. Lang, "which [to the nobles] was intolerable."[1] The Master of Gray was a Latin poet and friend of Sidney. Even Arran, whom the King liked though he did not trust, was a scholar and man of parts, though a rascal. "Avec du grec," wrote Hunsdon, "on ne peut gâter rien."[2]

The King's time in these years, according to Colville, was divided between hunting and poetry, "in one or both of which he commonly spendeth the day."[3] One can imagine far less profitable occupations in rainy weather and on winter nights around the fire. James, it is true, was not much of a poet, nor could he have been if he had had friends who were more capable of leading the way, but he had at least the quick and fertile mind of a good talker. At his meals, writes Walton later, there were "deep discourses" and "friendly disputes."[4] Sir John Harington pleased him as "a merry blade," but also for his fund of "learned discourse."[5] When James left Scotland in the hands of the Presbyterian clergy, the beginnings of the new poetry were soon lost in the concentration of interest in a sincere but unlovely religion, and verse was left for recluses such as Drummond or Scotsmen in the English court. The throne of the latter country might have been ascended, on the death of Glorianna, by a monarch less auspicious for literature than James I. And if, as Dr. McCrie has somewhere suggested, a proper fate would have been to force the King to live by his sonnets, he would have fared very badly in seventeenth-century Scotland.

[1] *History of Scotland*, Vol. II, p. 345.
[2] Letter to Burleigh, *ibid.*, p. 309.
[3] *Letters*, Bann. Club, p. 316.
[4] *Life of Donne*, ed. 1901, p. 207.
[5] *Nugæ Antiquæ*, ed. Park, p. 391.

IV

THE KING'S VERSE AND CRITICISM

"For such a poet, while thy days were green,
Thou wert, as chief of them are said t' have been."
— JONSON.

The discussion of the King's theory and practice of poetry is made appropriate at this point by the fact that most of his verse, as he remarks in the preface to the *Exercises at vacant houres*, was written in his "verie young and tender yeares: wherein nature, (except shee were a monster) can admit no perfection." All of his poems, save three or four sonnets and the revisions of his early paraphrases of the psalms, belong to the period of his reign in Scotland; and the greater portion of them were composed either before the publication of the first volume of his poems in his nineteenth year, or in the time of romantic enthusiasm excited by his marriage.

With this early verse should be connected the translations and sonnets of Montgomerie, Fowler, and the Hudsons, the whole representing an attempt, feeble indeed and abortive, to introduce new fashions of poetry into Scotland. In the little group which surrounded the King, there were frequent discussions of literary themes. Translations and paraphrases were planned and carried out. There were symposiums in which the excellence of the classical writers was considered, and the desirability of making it known to the "facound" wits of Scotland.[1]

---

[1] Cf. the quotation from Hudson, p. xxxv. Doubtless these dinner-table conversations were a development from the devotional reading which had accompanied his repasts from the time of his childhood. In an account of *The Present State of Scotland, 1586* (Roy. Hist. Soc., Vol. II, p. 262), it is recorded that there was a "chapter of the bible read with some exposition after each meal."

The manifesto of this minor Areopagus was the *Reulis and cautelis to be observit and eschewit in Scottis Poesie*,[1] and its sources and contents require first attention in a review of their work. "Sindrie hes written of it [the art of poetry] in English," says James vaguely, in the preface; but his indebtedness to Gascoigne's excellent *Notes of Instruction* (1575) is obvious on every page. The King and his guide in the art simply appropriated from the English treatise, after the fashion of border reivers, making adroit and somewhat disingenuous changes in order and phrasing, and adding or omitting as their tastes and the peculiarities of Scottish prosody suggested. On the other hand, the debt to French criticism is surprisingly slight, and confined to observations which are among the commonplaces of criticism early and late. Thus in his discussion of invention, and of art *vs.* nature (Preface and Chapter VII) James is closer to Horace[2] than to Ronsard; and in this and other matters he may owe something to the *Uranie* of Du Bartas, his translation of which is in the same volume with the *Reulis*. As a matter of fact, the *Défense* of Du Bellay and the *Abrégé de l'Art poétique* of Ronsard give scant attention to elementary matters of metrical technique, and it is with these that James is chiefly concerned.

When James warns poets to avoid matters of the commonweal, which "are to grave materis for a Poet to mell in," he is doubtless speaking from his experiences with the verse satirists of the Kirk party in Scotland. In other divergences from Gascoigne, the influence of Montgomerie is generally conspicuous. While Gascoigne would not have a poet "hunt the letter to death," James would use alliteration freely, and quotes in illustration a line from Montgomerie's highly alliterative *Flyting*. His recognition of proverbs, also, as one of the three special ornaments of

---

[1] The best edition is in *Elizabethan Critical Essays*, Vol. I, pp. 208–225. Professor Smith's notes indicate with sufficient fullness the debt to English and French criticism.

[2] Cf. *De Arte Poetica:* "Præstantissima est in omni arte, natura, et poetam non tam fieri, quam nasci sermone eruditorum dicitur."

verse, is doubtless suggested by their frequent occurrence in the writings of the "master poet." James is, I think, the only Elizabethan critic who explicitly condemns "rhymes-in-terms" (*e.g.* prove . . . disprove), and it is notable that the fault occurs but once in Montgomerie's poems and twice in his own (sonnets XXXIV and XXXVI). In all of these respects the practice of James conspicuously resembles that of the older poet. Of the quotations in the *Reulis*, three are from the author's own works, three unidentified, and seven from Montgomerie.

An examination of the treatise [1] shows that the King, as an apprentice in the divine art, is interested not so much in the high purposes of poetry as in details of verse-making and diction. While it is not enough, it is still his chief concern that a poem shall "flow well, with many pretie wordes." In matters of technique he prefers the definite and positive rule. The cesura must fall in the middle and must follow an accented syllable; there must be a pause at the end of every line; weak endings, faulty rhymes, misplaced accents are to be avoided. On all these points he is a stickler for metrical propriety. In his practice, though he cannot strictly obey his precepts, he is reasonably correct. But one of his sonnets contains more than five rhymes, albeit the difficulty of the scheme often contorts his syntax and renders his phrasing grotesque. While it is true that the *Reulis and cautelis* was the work of his boyhood, and was written at a time when the confusion of poetic standards made dogmatism desirable, while the scantiness of contemporary poetry made the establishment

---

[1] The most interesting portion of the *Reulis* is Chap. VIII, "tuiching the kyndis of versis." His application there of the term *verse heroicall* to a stanza of nine lines, *aab, aab, bab*, may explain Ludovick Briskett's statement, before 1589, that *The Faërie Queene* was written in heroicall verse (Spenser, Globe ed., p. xxxiv). His condemnation of the iambic pentameter, or heroic couplet, as "ryme quhilk servis onely for lang historeis, and yit are nocht verse," may perhaps be traced to Montgomerie's avoidance of the metre, or to Ronsard's remark that he preferred the Alexandrine, though he wrote *La Françiade* in pentameter at the desire of the King (Preface to *La Françiade. Œuvres*, ed. Marty-Lavaux, Vol. III, p. 516; and cf. *Abrégé*, Vol. VI, p. 455).

of final principles impossible, it is nevertheless quite likely that the King retained in later years his early precisian views. He had at least this trait of the pedant that he was fond of formulating principles and sticking to them regardless of facts or consequences, as may easily be seen by noting the conformity of many of the doctrines in the *Basilikon Doron* to the actual conduct of his government. Furthermore, Scottish versemen, from the northern Chaucerians to Drummond and even later, were more conscientious and often more successful metricians than their English contemporaries, and Montgomerie, the King's mentor, was especially adept. In the case of James, one may see the trend of his taste not only by his practice, but by his *Sonnet on Sir William Alexander's Harshe Verses after the Ingliche Fasone* (XLVI) and by his liking for *Forth Feasting*, the most correct of Drummond's polished verse. Whatever his direct influence, the King's tastes were on the side of formal accuracy.[1]

In turning to the King's actual accomplishment in verse, the early date of most of it should be borne in mind, and the fact that it was written when the influence of the old native poetry was nearly dead in Scotland, and when the new lyric impulse from abroad was just beginning to make itself felt. James corresponds in Scotland to the Elizabethan tentatives of the sixties, seventies, and eighties; and his amatory lyrics are not on a much lower level than the "fragrant flowers," "pleasant delites," and "daynty devises" which represent the average of the miscellanies from *Tottel's* to the *Phœnix Nest* of 1583. It is a mistake to think

[1] A less elementary discussion of style in verse and prose occurs in the *Basilikon Doron*, where it has attracted less attention, though parts of it are quoted in Mr. Rait's introduction to the volume entitled *A Royal Rhetorician*, London, 1900. The chief points in James's remarks are that prose should be plain and short, but stately; that one's work should be passed to others for criticism; that a poem should be "so rich in quicke inventions, and poeticke flowers, and in faire and pertinent comparisons, as it shall retaine the lustre of a poem, although in prose"; and that "since there is nothing left to be saide in Greeke and Latine alreadie, and ynew of poore schollers would match you in these languages, . . . it best becometh a King to purify and make famous his own tongue, wherein he may go before all his subjects."

of James as a Jacobean and not as a belated Elizabethan, or to judge his work by more severe standards than those applied to the lyrics of Gascoigne and Googe or the translations of Golding and Phaer.

Like the work of the last-mentioned writers, James's translations from Du Bartas are in fourteeners, and whatever poetical beauty they may have had for contemporary ears [1] is greatly diminished for modern readers by the lilt and flop of this almost fatal measure. The translations are further weakened by the crabbed literalness with which they follow the original. Even in the King's own invention in the same metre, *The Lepanto,* Dr. Irving searches vainly for "felicity of expression or elevation of thought." [2] Graces such as he implies are truly lacking, but James, as in his prose and conversation, had a gift of picturesque and racy phrase. His style in the description of the battle between the Christian and the Turkish navies is concrete and lively, and at times achieves an almost ballad-like simplicity, as in the account of the gathering of the Christian forces, ll. 268–279 : —

> "There came eight thousand Spaniards brave,
>   From hotte and barren Spaine,
> Good order kepars, cold in fight,
>   With proud disdainfull braine.
> From pleasant fertill Italie,
>   There came twelve thousand als,
> With subtill spreites bent to revenge,
>   By craftie meanes and fals.
> Three thousande Almans also came,
>   From Countries colde and wide,
> These monney men with awfull cheare
>   The chok will dourelie bide."

The *Dreame on his Mistris* (XVII) is perhaps a better example of the author's ability to handle "eights and

---

[1] Gascoigne says Phaer's *Virgil* is "in a brave long verse, stately and flowing. . . ." — *Eliz. Critical Essays*, Vol. I, p. 362.

[2] *History of Scotish Poetry*, p. 502.

sixes" with some approach to dignity. This and the *Complaint of his Mistressis Absence from Court* (XVI) were written some years later than the other pieces of the *Amatoria*, and show the progress he was making toward a sounder conception of poetry. They are not, like most of the early poems, a mere jumble of fantastic conceits. They are chiefly commendable, however, the first poem for the ingenious comparison of the alteration at court to changed weather at sea, and the second for the skill with which the poet interprets the tokens left by his mistress. Like the *Phœnix*, an allegorical elegy on the death of d'Aubigny (*Essayes of a Prentise*), the *Satire against Woemen* (XVIII), and the *Admonition* (LI), the two pieces display a cleverness of invention which somewhat atones for the absence of more poetical qualities.

In his short poems, the King's favorite form is the sonnet, a form suited, according to the *Reulis and cautelis*, not only for love matters, but for the "compendious praysing of any bukes, or the authoris thairof, or any argumentis of uther historeis"; and the rhyme-scheme he adopts is of especial interest in connection with the practice of contemporary writers. Hoffmann[1] has already pointed out that the arrangement of the rhymes in Spenser's *Amoretti*, *abab*, *bcbc*, *cdcd*, *ee*, was employed also by Montgomerie in thirty-seven of his seventy-two sonnets, and that one of these was published in *The Essayes of a Prentise* in 1584, the first appearance of the form in print.[2] But it is notable that the King and the other sonneteers in the *Essayes* adopt the same scheme, and that James adheres to it strictly in all save four of his published sonnets. Little significance need be attached to the actual date of publication, and Spenser must have written sonnets — other than the unrhymed translations from Petrarch and Du Bellay — earlier than

[1] *Englische Studien*, Vol. XX, p. 24.

[2] It is not true, as has sometimes been stated, that the final couplet is unknown in French sonnets. To be specific, five of Ronsard's, three of Du Bellay's, one of Jodelle's, two of Dorat's, and eight of Thyard's have the couplet; and two of Ronsard's have alternate rhymes in the octave as well as the sestet.

1586;[1] but he is not known to have published any before
the dedicatory verses at the opening of *The Faërie Queene* in
1590,[2] and by this time he would have been familiar with
the King's reputation as a patron, and doubtless also with
his verse. It is not in any case a matter to be settled by
the relative merits of the writers concerned. Either James
or Montgomerie, with their fondness for intricate and frequent rhyming, might have invented the scheme by following Gascoigne's statement that "the first twelve [lines] do
ryme in staves of four lines by crosse meetre, and the last
two ryming togither do conclude the whole."[3]

Daniel is the only English poet who adopts the rhyming
of Spenser in any of his sonnets;[4] but it is found more frequently among Scottish writers, and is in such cases a sign
of the influence of James and Montgomerie. The Hudsons
and Fowler employ it exclusively in the scanty collections
of their verse which have survived; there are five or six
examples scattered among the poems of Sir William Alexander[5] and Sir David Murray;[6] Mure of Rowallan[7] uses
it in twenty-five or thirty sonnets. In Scotland it is frequently the form adopted by occasional and amateur prac-
titioners,[8] often with a view apparently of pleasing the King.

[1] A sonnet to Harvey (Globe ed., p. 607) is dated July 18, of this year.

[2] It has often been noticed that the Spenserian stanza is precisely the first
nine lines of the Spenserian sonnet, with an additional foot at the end. One
might easily, therefore, have been developed from the other. If, however,
the stanza is to be traced to others of similar length, it should be compared,
not with *ottava rima*, which Spenser employs nowhere save in *Muiopotmos*,
but with the French octave, *abab, bcbc*, which he uses frequently. This was
even more popular in Scottish poetry than in English, and was one of the
favorite staves of Scott, Maitland, Montgomerie, and other contemporaries
of James.

[3] *Elizabethan Critical Essays*, Vol. I, p. 55.

[4] In eight sonnets, *Works*, ed. Grosart, Vol. I, pp. 17, 35, 49, 59, 60, 223,
277.

[5] *Works*, ed. 1870–1872, Vol. I, pp. 38, 46. For another by Aytoun, cf.
p. xxix.

[6] *Poems*, Bann. Club, XV and XVIII of the sonnets to *Cœlia*. Also a
commendatory sonnet by Simon Grahame prefixed to *Sophonisba*.

[7] *Works*, S. T. S., Vol. I, pp. 47–58, 301–306.

[8] Among others, three sonnets by James Melville in *Vita et Morte Roberti
Rollok*, Bann. Club reprint; six by Walter Quin on the heroes of the Gowry

The latter's persistent use of it in spite of its difficulty may indicate that he took some credit to himself for its inception; it at least shows his attention to matters of form. Of the five sonnets with inclosed instead of alternate rhymes, one, the fifth of the *Amatoria*, is written with a pretense of anonymity, and the rest are of much later date.[1] An examination of all the sonnets shows that more than half make the 'turn' at the end of the eighth instead of the twelfth line, though several are arranged as a series of quatrains with a final couplet.

It would be easy to illustrate from the poems the sins of the school of conceits, as for instance in the sonnet on the Armada (App. II, II), where the storm which aided in the defeat of the Spanish navy is attributed to the boisterous laughter of God, or the passage of the *Uranie*, quoted on page xxxv, in which the Bible is likened, among other things, to a bottomless ocean, a spring of eloquence, and a cornucopia. Here the author is following Du Bartas, whose influence on his British followers, whatever his original merits, must be considered wholly pernicious. As a final instance may be cited the sonnet on Archbishop Adamson's paraphrase of Job, which is spun entirely out of the supposed resemblance between the prelate's "gifts of sprite" and Job's "gifts of geare."

James is most nearly inspired on the subject of the divine right of kings; the sonnet to Henry at the beginning of the *Basilikon Doron* (App. II, V) opens with the finely Tamburlanian line, —

"God gives not Kings the stile of Gods in vaine,"

and maintains something of this high and stately dignity throughout. Three other sonnets, written towards the close of the King's reign in Scotland, are easily distinguished from the rest as the summit of his achievement in poetry.

Fray in *Sertum Poeticum*, Edinburgh, 1600; one by Alexander Hume, *Poems*, S. T. S., p. 9; and a large number by Alexander Craig in his *Poeticall Essayes*, London, 1604, and *Poeticall Recreations*, Edinburgh, 1609.

[1] In the present collection, XXXIV, XLVII, XLIX, and App. II, IV.

One of these is the *Ænigme of Sleepe* (XXXVI), more pleasing in thought than in style, yet not unworthy of comparison with better-known essays on this familiar theme. The other two are the pair of sonnets on page 39, the first beginning,

"Not orientall Indus cristall streames,"

and the second,

"Faire famous Isle, where Agathocles rang."

In sustained music, conformity to the technique of the sonnet, and prettiness of fancy, if not elevation, these might find a place in even a limited anthology of the sonnets of the sixteenth and early seventeenth centuries.

A minor poet is fortunate if he has thus surpassed himself in two or three poems. Yet in the case of James, while it is hardly necessary to apply Sir James Melville's remark regarding Mary Stuart's lute playing, that she did "reasonably for a queen," it is still true that his verse derives its interest chiefly from his high political station and the consequent value attached to an intimate revelation of his personal character. In this respect, his poems do not reflect the vices and extreme feebleness of which he is often accused. They show, however, that though of an emotional temperament — quick to tears or laughter — James was blessed with little imagination or insight. Such gifts as he had were more distinctly intellectual — an orderly and inventive habit of mind, agility in debate, and a fondness for logical finesse which had been cultivated from his school days under Buchanan, who was himself both controversialist and poet.

The formula of his verse would include as important elements the extravagant style of Renaissance love poetry, imitated chiefly from Montgomerie; the limitations of theme and treatment due to his exalted position and his acceptance of the narrow views of Calvinism; and the tendency toward intellectual activity uncontrolled by good sense which was not uncommon in current discussions of politics and religion. The first and last of these influences are conspicuous in Jacobean poetry; and it might even be said that, though his work belongs to an earlier period, his training and tastes were fairly in accord with those which prevailed during his reign in England.

V

ARRIVAL IN ENGLAND: PATRONAGE OF PROSE AND THE DRAMA

"The very poets with their idle pamphlets, promise themselves large part in his favour."

James's reputation as a poet and patron reached England long before his accession to the throne, and heightened the chorus of welcome on his actual arrival. Sidney's mention of "King James of Scotland"[1] as patron of poetry undoubtedly refers to the author of *The Kingis Quair*, though if the *Apology* were written as late as 1583 Sidney must have been aware of the younger Stuart's scholarly accomplishments. Ten years later both of James's early volumes of verse were evidently familiar to Harvey, who devotes a paragraph of *Pierce's Supererogation* to euphuistic praise of Du Bartas and the King — "the woorthy Prince that is a Homer to himselfe, a Golden spurre to Nobility, a Scepter to Vertue, a verdure to the Spring, a Sunne to the day, and hath not onely translated the two diuine Poems of Salustius du Bartas, his Heavenly Vrany, and his hellish Furies, but hath readd a most valorous Martial Lecture unto himself in his owne victorious Lepanto, a short, but heroicall worke, in meeter, but royall meeter, fitt for a Dauids harpe."[2]

Barnfield, in 1598, makes the King's love of poetry the point of the second sonnet at the opening of his *Poems: in divers Humors :*[3] —

"And you, that discommend sweet Poesie,
(So that the Subject of the same be good)

---

[1] *Elizabethan Critical Essays*, ed. Gregory Smith, Vol. I, p. 193. For Sidney's intercourse with James, cf. XXX, note.

[2] *Ibid.*, Vol. II, p. 265. [3] Roxburghe Club ed., p. 181.

Here may you see, your fond simplicitie,
Sith Kings have favored it, of royal Blood.
The King of Scots (now living) is a Poet
As his Lepanto and his Furies show it."

Meres, in *Palladis Tamia* (1598), quotes the last two lines
of Barnfield,[1] while Vaughan in *The Golden Grove* (1600)
writes that "James . . . is a notable Poet, and daily
setteth out most learned poems, to the admiration of all
his subjects."[2]

In Allott's *England's Parnassus* (1600),[3] there are ten
quotations from James, nine from the *Uranie* and one from
the *Phœnix*, amounting in all to about seventy lines. Bodenham in his account of the contributors to *Belvedére, or
The Garden of the Muses*,[4] published in the same year, gives
to James a place of honor. He has drawn, he writes, first
from the triumphs, tiltings, and similar laudatory verses
dedicated to Elizabeth; and next from "what workes of
Poetrie have been put to the world's eye by that learned
and right royall king and Poet, James King of Scotland, no
one sentence of worth hath escaped. . . ." The number
of lines which passed this test are not easily discovered in
the olla-podrida of Bodenham's collection.

It was thus with a well-justified hope "of a more regard
to the present condition of our writings, in respect of our
soveraignes happy inclination this way,"[5] that poets good,
bad and indifferent lifted up their voices in mingled grief and
rejoicing at the change of rulers. Innumerable were the
"Sorrowes Joyes" and "Mournefull Ditties to a pleasant
newe Note" which met the King on his leisurely progress
into England. Daniel, Drayton, T. Greene the actor, the
two Fletchers of Cambridge in the poems issued by the
University, Chettle the playwright, were among the more

---

[1] *Elizabethan Critical Essays*, ed. Smith, Vol. II, p. 321.
[2] *Ibid.*, p. 326.
[3] Collier's *Poetical Miscellanies*, Vol. VI; and on the authorship of quotations, cf. Crawfurd, *Notes and Queries*, Ser. X, Vol. X, p. 262.
[4] Spenser Society reprint, London, 1875.
[5] From the prefatory note of Daniel's *Defence of Ryme* (1603).

conspicuous who thus mingled dirge and panegyric.[1] To gratify fully the hopes of these poets, the royal revenues must needs have exceeded the bounds of their imaginations. But there is good evidence that James, with his characteristic recklessness in money matters, and after the 'patterns of vertuous princes' he had studied in childhood, seriously intended to take the arts and letters under his protection.

In this respect it was not difficult for him to surpass the generosity of his predecessor, regarding whom the best Vaughan can say is that she made a certain Dr. Haddon master of requests.[2] Indeed, though the Queen's person and career stirred her subjects to high poetical enthusiasm, there is little to show that she was particularly interested in literature or extended assistance of a more practical sort. Patronage during her reign came chiefly from gentlemen of culture such as Sidney and Essex, and from noble ladies such as Sidney's sister the Countess of Pembroke, the Countess of Cumberland and her mother, and the Countess of Bedford.[3]

Under James, this private encouragement was supplemented and in some measure supplanted by the direct support of the royal family. This may be accounted for not only by the royal monopoly of dramatic patronage, but also by the King's personal interest in poetry and prose controversy, Shakspere's position as chief dramatist of the King's company of actors, Bacon's political promotion, Donne's preferment in the church by the King's influence, and Jonson's services as composer of masques illustrate, not so much the rewards extended for literary accomplishment, as the relations with the court of the chief literary figures of the period.

The general question of court patronage of the drama in the reign of James is much too complicated for brief or sub-

---

[1] For poems on the accession, cf. Nichols, *Progresses of King James*, Vol. I, pp. x–xxxvii.

[2] *Elizabethan Critical Essays*, Vol. II, p. 325.

[3] Cf. Miss Ph. Sheavyn, *Patrons and Professional Writers under Elizabeth and James I*. In discussing the incomes of writers, Miss Sheavyn makes but slight reference to gifts and pensions from the crown.

ordinated treatment, and has been left outside the scope of
the present study. Attention may be called merely to the
King's early interest in entertainments of this character, an
interest which may explain the pleasure which in later years
he is known to have taken in all forms of drama and the-
atrical spectacle. The evidence on this point is furnished
in part by the masque or *Epithalamion* (LIV) which he
himself contrived in 1588 for the marriage of his ward, the
daughter of Lennox, and the Earl of Huntly. Save as
the sole extant example of its type in Scottish literature,
the piece is in no way remarkable, and mingles disguise,
dialogue, spectacle, comic byplay (at least suggested by the
presence of the zany or clown), and classical mythology
after the usual formula of French Hymenée and English
maskings at feasts and royal progresses. Though there is
no indication of dancing, the component elements are otherwise much the same as those of the more elaborate shows of
Jonson and Inigo Jones, at which it is only fair to suppose
the King an appreciative spectator, capable of enjoying
not merely the fantastic erudition of the pieces, but also
their finer artistic and poetic qualities.[1]

James had a hand also, with his friend William Fowler, in
the games and shows at the christening of Prince Henry,
August 23, 1594. The entertainment at the banquet following the ceremony, according to Fowler,[2] was intended
by the King as an allegory representing the favor shown

---

[1] There is thus no reason for accepting Brotanek's suggestion that the
popularity of the masque in the English court was due chiefly to the influence of Queen Anne, or that it was unknown in England prior to her arrival.
(*Die Englische Maskenspiele, Wiener Beiträge,* 1902, p. 279.)

[2] *A True Accompt . . . of the baptism of . . . Prince Henry,* Edinburgh,
1594(?). Printed, from the London edition of 1603, in Nichols, *Progresses of
Eliz.,* Vol. III, pp. 353-369. At a second banquet a chariot was employed,
on which was a table surrounded by six ladies, — Ceres, Faith, Fecundity,
Concord, Liberty, and Perseverance. It was to have been drawn in by a
tame lion (who figures in the treasurer's accounts of the time), but this experiment was abandoned "lest his presence might have brought some fear to
the nearest." Malone has connected this with the lion in *Midsummer
Night's Dream* (*c.* 1594), whose roaring "might fright the duchess and the
ladies." The existence of a 1594 edition of the *Accompt,* of which Malone
was unaware, makes his suggestion not unlikely.

him by the gods during his voyage to Denmark and in the
happy issue of his marriage. Its chief property consisted
of a movable ship, eighteen feet long, eight feet wide, and
four feet high, which was elaborately decorated with sails
of taffeta, ordnance, and rigging, and manned by Arion
with his harp, Neptune, Thetis, and Triton, three sirens,
six sailors, and fourteen musicians. The vessel approached
the table, delivered the banquet, and departed at the close
after the singing of the *One Hundred Twenty-eighth Psalm*.
The whole entertainment, of which this was merely a
part, and which extended over several days, illustrates the
pleasure taken by the royal couple in gorgeous and costly
spectacle.

These, however, were but the pastimes of idle moments.
Of a much more serious character was the King's interest
in the disputes of scholars over problems in theology and in
what was at the time the closely allied subject of the theory
of government. From his childhood his studies had been
especially in these fields; as the French Ambassador,
Boderie, remarks, theology was the subject which he knew
best, and in the discussion of which he took the greatest
pleasure.[1] The sermons and paraphrases in the stirring
years of Spanish preparations against England have already
been mentioned.[2] The *Dæmonologie*, a dialogue on witchcraft, directed especially against the damnable scepticism of
Reginald Scott and the German physician Weirus, appeared
in 1597; *The Trewe Lawe of free [i.e.* absolute] *Monarchies*,[3]
in answer to the arguments of Buchanan, Hotman, Hubert
Languet, and similar reformers, in 1598; and the *Basilikon
Doron*, altogether the most original and pleasing of the
King's writings, early in 1599.[4] The curiosity aroused by
James's accession to the English throne led to the republi-

---

[1] *Ambassades*, ed. 1750, Vol. III, p. 190.
[2] Cf. p. xxxiv.
[3] "The bent of it was directed against the course of God's worke in our
Kirk and ellis where, as rebellious to Kings." — Calderwood, *Historie of the
Kirk of Scotland*, Vol. V, p. 727.
[4] The first edition was limited to seven copies. Nicholson refers to the
treatise in a letter written in October, 1598 (*Cal. S. P. Sco.*, p. 759).

cation of all of these in or about the year 1603, and the translation of the more important into Latin, French, and other languages.

After a short interval, the King was again stirred to controversy by Catholic opposition to the Oath of Allegiance (1606), following the Gunpowder Plot, which required Catholic Englishmen to deny the temporal supremacy of the Pope. *An Apologie For The Oath of Allegiance*, which appeared late in 1607,[1] was the King's defense of this requirement, in reply especially to two *breves* from the Pope to English Catholics and Cardinal Bellarmine's published letter to the Archpriest George Blackwell.[2] The *Apologie* was re-issued in May, 1609,[3] with formal admission of the royal authorship and an extended *Premonition To All Most Mightie Monarches, Kings, Free Princes, and States of Christendome*, defending the *Apologie* against its critics. In the meantime a veritable battle of the books had ensued, in which continental theologians found a target for their pamphlets in the prominence of their royal opponent. Before 1615 at least thirty-six distinct works appeared on one side or the other, and a complete list of translations, re-issues, and skirmishes on the borders of the main engagement would number many more.[4] Among the more important English writers who came to the King's defense were Launcelot Andrewes, Bishop of Chichester, William Barlow, Bishop of Lincoln, William Tooker, Dean of Lichfield, John Donne the poet, John Barclay, and Samuel Collins, Regius Professor at Cambridge. "On y travaille," writes Boderie of the *Premonition*, "et il y a une petite congrégation

[1] "Il se trouvera du bien et du mal . . . le style en est vehement et temoigne de la passion." — Boderie, Vol. II, p. 105 (December, 1607).

[2] Cf. W. H. Frere, *A History of the English Church in the Reigns of Elizabeth and James I*, London, 1904, pp. 337 ff.

[3] *Hist. MSS. Comm. Reports*, IV, p. 343. Letter written by W. Johnson, May 24, 1609, sending a book "lately set forth by the King, presently called in again, and now newly set forth . . . out of the press but yesterday."

[4] A list, by no means complete, is given by Birch in an appendix to the 1772 edition of Harris's *Life and Writings of James I*. For a more extended account of the King's part in the controversy, cf. Irving, *Lives of the Scotish Poets*, Vol. II, pp. 232–251.

de gens doctes qui tous les jours s'assemblent devant le dit Roi, pou revoir et corriger les traductions qui en ont été faites." [1]   Their method evidently was the same as that employed by the contemporary translators of the Bible. In 1612, the King gave a new turn to the discussion by the publication of *A Declaration concerning the Proceedings with the States Generall, of the United Provinces of the Low Countreys, in the cause of D. Conradus Vorstius,* an attack on the Dutch professor for his Arminian disbelief in the limited essence and complete foreknowledge of God.   The main question was again taken up, however, in *A Remonstrance for the Right of Kings, and the Independance of their Crownes, against an Oration of the Most Illustrious Card. of Perron, pronounced in the Chamber of the third Estate, Jan. 15, 1615.* In the next year, all of these prose pieces, with six of the King's addresses in Parliament, were gathered together in chronological order in a single folio volume.

The almost complete oblivion of these tracts, in modern times, obscures somewhat their importance in the age when they were written.   They were the defense of the established monarchical form of government, on the one hand against the Puritans who in Scotland and later in England sought to set up a religious commonwealth like that of Calvin at Geneva, and on the other hand against the pretensions of the Pope to temporal power.   Like Hooker in the reign of Elizabeth, James bent his energies to meet these attacks; and however extreme his position, it was fundamentally in accord with what has remained the traditional English attitude.   The theory of the divine right of kings was now first fully formulated; fantastic as it may seem to-day, it was the result merely of an effort to find for monarchy the same sanction as that asserted by its opponents, and the only one they were disposed to accept.   Needless to say, if James could have conducted his government as skilfully as his arguments, such defense might not have been necessary.

In the partial list, already given, of writers whom re-

---

[1] *Ambassades,* Vol. IV, p. 323 (May 14, 1609).

ligious zeal or desire for royal favor drew into this ink and paper warfare, the names of Donne and Barclay[1] are the only ones of much note in literature. For the latter's stay in England, and his services as the King's literary assistant and companion in scholarship, his biographers have hitherto depended largely on the references in his own writings and those of his friend Casaubon; but these may easily be supplemented by the records, in part given in the calendars of state papers, of the place and pension which he received for his reward. Barclay's father was a Scottish Catholic who in the reign of Mary had settled at Pont-à-Mousson as professor of law in a Jesuit college, and who as a Catholic had attracted attention in 1600 by a treatise defending the rights of kings against the Pope.[2] Father and son paid a short visit to England in 1603, and in 1606 the son was again in London, seeking patronage in the usual fashion by the composition of adulatory verses in Latin.[3] His first recorded recompense was £100, paid by Cecil, October 26, 1607,[4] and in the following June he was granted an annuity of £250.[5]

The date of his second departure from England and the nature of his mission abroad may be derived from a letter of Boderie, June 24, 1609, to the effect that Barclay had been appointed to carry the *Premonition* to the Emperor of Germany, the King of Hungary, and the Dukes of

---

[1] John Barclay (1582–1621) is remembered chiefly as the author of *Euphormionis Satyricon* (1603), one of the first examples of picaresque fiction outside of Spain, and of *Argenis* (1621), a widely read ideal romance in Latin, with allusions to contemporary courts and politics. Cf. *Cam. Hist. of Eng. Lit.*, Vol. IV, Chap. xiii, and references there cited.

[2] *De Regno et regali potestate, adversos Buchanum, Brutum, et Boucherium, et reliquos Monarchomachos*, Paris, 1600.

[3] His poems entitled *Sylvæ* (London, 1606) are dedicated to Christian IV of Denmark, who visited England in July of that year. They contain verses to James, on the rumor of his death (March 24, 1606), and to Prince Henry, Cecil, Lennox, and Hay.

[4] *Cal. S. P. Dom.*

[5] "An annuity of 250 li. per anno for John Barklay gent. stranger, for terme of his lyfe, to beginne from our Lady day last past." — *Signet Office Docquets*, Public Records Office. (References to the original documents indicate that the payments do not appear in the calendars.)

Bavaria, Lorraine, and Savoy.[1] For this journey a payment had already been made, May 29, "unto his Ma[ties] servants [John] Barclay and Robert Aytoun [the poet] gents. and of the Grooms of the Privy Chamber the sum of 300 li. to each of them, for their charge and expense, being sent unto divers forraine Princes with His M[s] L'res";[2] and in November Barclay obtained £200 in addition.[3] Later grants and gifts[4] may be recorded briefly as follows: January, 1610, pension of £200, on surrender of his former pension of £250[3]; February, 1611, pension of £60 to Anne de Malaville, wife of William Barclay;[2] July, 1611, free gift of £100[3]; March, 1614, pension of £200 to Louise Barclay, wife of John Barclay;[2] August, 1615, "to John Barklay, Esq., the sum of 250 li. of his Ma[ties] free gift, in consideration of his services."[2] At the time of this last payment, Barclay seems to have been making preparations for his final change of residence to Rome, where he spent the last years of his life, for in this year he gathered together a second volume of poems, and there is a record of a transfer to a financial agent named Burlamachi of all three of the pensions which had been granted to him and his family.[5]

In return for these rewards, Barclay assisted the King in translation[6] and in search for authorities,[7] published his

[1] *Ambassades*, Vol. IV, p. 376.

[2] *Signet Office Docquets.*

[3] *Cal. S. P. Dom.*

[4] September 2, 1610, he was seeking the grant of an escheat which had been promised him by the King; and December 21, 1611, he wrote Cecil from Paris for the payment of his pension. — *Cal. S. P. Dom.*

[5] September, 1615, "An annuity of 260 li. for Phillip Burlamacni during his life upon surrender of two several annuities, one of 200 li. granted to John Barclay, gent. stranger, and the other of 60 li. granted to Anne de Malaville widow of a William Barclay during her life. And also the grant of one other annuity of 200 li. . . . upon surrender of the like annuity granted to Louise Barclay, wife of John Barclay, after the disease of her said husband." — *Docquets.*

[6] "Sir Henry Seville is appointed to correct the translation of the King's book, which was first done by Davies, then by Lionel Sharpe, by Wilson, and last by Barclay the French poet." — Chamberlaine to Carleton, April 27, 1609, *Cal. S. P. Dom.*

[7] In the Bodl. MS. of the *Premonition* there is a note in the King's hand, "to remember to speak with barclaye." — *Lusus Regius*, p. x.

father's *De Potestate Papæ* (1609), answered the critics
of this work in his *Pietas* (1612), and served especially
as a companion for the King in the learned discussions
in which he delighted. "Ad Regem hodie Genovicum
profectus," writes Casaubon, June, 1614, "cum eruditis-
simo et amicissimo Barclaio diem suavissime consumpsi." [1]
Casaubon was fond of such kindly superlatives, but
there is evidence that even he at times grew weary of
the continued attendance which James was pleased to
require.

Walton, in his life of Donne, gives an account of the similar manner in which the English poet gained a standing at
court: "The King had formerly both known and put a
value upon his company, and had also given him some hopes
of a state-employment; being always much pleased when
Mr. Donne attended him, especially at his meals, where
there were usually many deep discourses of general learning
and very often friendly disputes, or debates of religion betwixt his Majesty and those divines whose places required
their attendance on him.[2] According to Mr. Gosse,[3] though
this pleasant story is doubtless true of a later period, there
is no evidence of talk at meals or other intercourse between
Donne and James prior to 1614, save on one occasion in
1609 — again recorded by Walton — when the King commanded the composition of the *Pseudo-Martyr*. It is indeed true that such court favor as the poet had, assisted
him little in his futile efforts during the years 1607–1610
for such posts as Sir William Fowler's office of secretary

---

[1] *Ephemerides*, ed. Russell, p. 1062. Casaubon came to England early in
1611, and remained as the King's pensioner until his death in 1614. His
opinions of his patron in his diary and private letters are uniformly favorable.
He found him "greater than report, and thought him more so every time
he saw him." — *Ephem.* "I enjoy the favor of this excellent monarch, who
is really more instructed than most people give him credit for. He is a lover
of learning to a degree beyond belief; his judgement of books, old and new,
is such as would become a professed scholar rather than a mighty prince." —
Letter to the historian De Thou. (The passages are quoted and translated
in Pattison, *Isaac Casaubon*, ed. 1892, pp. 695, 285.)

[2] *Life of Donne*, Library of English Classics, p. 207.

[3] *The Life and Letters of John Donne*, London, 1899, Vol. II, p. 58.

to the Queen,[1] a secretaryship in Ireland, and the place George Sandys later occupied as secretary in Virginia. Yet, even in this earlier period, it is inconceivable that James, who was on the lookout for clever young scholars and waverers from Catholicism, was not aware of Donne's gifts and search for preferment. Thomas Morton, whom Donne had assisted in controversy, was in 1607 one of the King's chaplains-in-ordinary; Sir Henry Goodyer, to whom the poet for years sent weekly letters, was of the privy chamber; Sir Robert Ker, another friend, was in the Prince's household. If the *Pseudo-Martyr* was not written at the King's command — and of course such authority would not in any case be spoken of in the book itself — it was at least dedicated to the King and written chiefly to win his regard. When, in November, 1614, the poet's claims were finally presented definitely to James, he evidently had already formed an opinion of Donne's gifts and a plan for his career: "I know Mr. Donne is a learned man, has the abilities of a learned Divine, and will prove a powerful preacher; and my desire is to prefer him that way, and in that way I will deny you nothing for him." [2] The idea of entering the church had been in Donne's mind at least two or three years earlier; and if, as he used to say later, the King "first inclined him to be a minister," there may possibly have been some previous offer, hindered, as Mr. Gosse would suggest, by the poet's hesitation on points of doctrine.

Walton states that soon after his entering the church Donne became one of the King's chaplains; he at least preached frequently at court and pleased the King greatly by his sermons. "A piece of such perfection as could admit neither addition nor diminution," James is said to

---

[1] *Ibid.*, Vol. I, p. 156. Mr. Gosse here suggests that Donne was seeking merely some employment under Fowler; but that his aim was the secretary-ship itself is shown by a reference in a letter to Goodyer in 1611: "And for a token of my desire to serve him, present Mr. Fowler with three or four thousand pounds of this, since he was so resolved never to leave his place without a suit of like value." — *Ibid.*, Vol. I, p. 240.

[2] Walton, *Life of Donne*, p. 208.

have remarked of the *Instructions to Preachers*, printed at his desire in 1622.[1]   Donne's paraphrase of the five opening chapters of the *Lamentations* of Jeremiah belongs to an unfortunate type of poetry, the fashion of which was encouraged by the example of the King; and it may not be rash to suggest that the smoother rhythm which Mr. Gosse notes in his poems after 1615, — the "abandonment of the harsh and eccentric inversions of his earlier manner, so marked as to be in itself an indication of the period when a poem was composed," [2] — was in some degree a concession to the orthodox taste of his friends at court and his royal master.

[1] Gosse, *Life and Letters of John Donne*, Vol. II, p. 161.
[2] *Ibid.*, Vol. II, p. 76.

VI

POETS IN THE ENGLISH COURT, 1603–1625

"He leades the lawlesse poets of our times,
To smoother cadence, to exacter rimes."
— Sir John Beaumont, *To the Glorious
Memory of . . . King James.*

Of the two writers considered in the preceding chapter, Barclay held the rank of a groom of the privy chamber, and Donne, according to Walton, was one of the King's chaplains-in-ordinary. In general, patronage during the reign — aside from small gifts for dedications — was distributed in this way, either by means of a pension or a place in one of the households into which the court was divided. The royal family lived much apart; the establishments of the King and the Queen, of Prince Henry (prior to his death, November 6, 1612), and of Prince Charles (after his creation, November 4, 1616), were distinct from each other, and separate accounts were kept of wages, fees, annuities, and similar disbursals. A pension or even a nominal position in one of the households meant that the holder, if he were a man of letters, would regard its head as his special patron, to whom tribute in the form of verse or dedication might properly be directed, and would be in a kind of family relationship with others in the same service.

THE COURT OF PRINCE HENRY

Prince Henry's household was established immediately after his arrival from Scotland, and before the end of 1603 numbered one hundred forty-one members, fifty-six above stairs and eighty-five below.[1]   At its head was Sir Thomas Chaloner, formerly an English agent abroad, and in Scotland during the winter preceding the death of Elizabeth. He was a gentleman of scholarly parts, author of one of the elegies in Sylvester's *Lachrymæ Lachrymarum* on the death of Henry, and in his later years interested especially in scientific studies.   Adam Newton, the Prince's tutor, acted as secretary; and Sir David Murray, who like others of his kindred seems to have possessed both practical and poetical talents, was groom of the stole and keeper of the privy purse.

It was the King's wish, expressed to Chaloner when he first signed his book, that " the forme of the Prince's house should rather imitate a colledge then a court," [2] by which he must have meant that it should be given to scholarly pursuits and composed in part of students and men of culture. To this policy may be due in some measure his son's reputation as a friend of the arts, though as he grew older the Prince himself showed the benefits of his excellent training by a personal interest in literature and by the expenditure of large sums for books and pictures.

Another reason for the modern favorable opinion of the Prince in this respect is the preservation of a detailed record of all his gifts, purchases, and other expenditures during the last four years of his life.   These are contained in two account books of Sir David Murray, one among the *Declared Accounts*, Pipe Office, Roll 2794, and the other among the *Exchequer Accounts*, Bundle 433, No. 8.   The first of these, entitled "The Accompte of the Money Expended by Sir David Murray K^t Keaper of the Privie Purse to the late Noble Prynce Henry, Prynce of Wales, from the first of October 1610 to the sixth of November

---

[1] T. Birch, *Life of Henry Prince of Wales*, London, 1760, p. 32.   Its size increased rapidly, until at the Prince's creation in 1610 there were 426 in the household, 297 with wages and 129 without (*Archeologia*, Vol. XII, p. 8). Positions were often bartered and distributed without much regard for the wishes of Henry or his immediate guardians.

[2] *An Account of the Revenues of . . . Prince Henry, Archeologia*, Vol. XV, p. 22.

1612 (the daye of the decease of the said Prynce) as lyke-
wise for certaine paymentes made after the deathe of the
saide Prynce in the monethes of November and December
1612," is given I think completely, though with changes
in the order and errors in the amounts of the payments, in
Cunningham's *Extracts from the Accounts of the Revels at
Court.*[1] It is a pleasant and illuminating record of the
Prince's pastimes and studies, his expenditures for jewels,
horses, plays, tiltings, books and paintings, "guyftes and
rewardes." The chief items of literary interest are gifts of
£30 to "Mr. Owen the latyne poett," of £10 to "Mr. Cory-
att," and pensions to "Mr. Silvester at xx li. per ann. [for
two years] . . . xl li.," and to "Mr. Drayton a poett for
one yeare . . . x li."[2] It need not cause surprise that the
payments for tennis balls were over three times as great as
the sums spent in support of literature; it might be shown
that the expenditures of his royal father for his "privie
buckehoundes" during any one year would have kept alive
all the worthy poets in London for the same length of time.

The second of Murray's books, preserved among the
Exchequer Accounts, bears the heading, "The Accounts of
Sir David Murray, Master of the Robes to Prince Henry,
from June 24, 1608 – September 29, 1609." So far as the
writer is aware, no extracts from this have been printed.
It has a special value, since, with the account printed by
Cunningham, it is the fullest record of the patronage of any
member of the royal family. One may infer from it that,
if we had Sir John Murray's records of the King's privy
purse, we should find frequent payments to scholars and
needy poets. The following extracts are the only ones in
any way connected with books or writers : —

July 13, 1608. To one who presented a booke to
his highnes contayning all the walkes and
parkes of Windsor . . . . 5 li.

---

[1] Shakespeare Society, 1842, Introd., pp. vii–xviii.

[2] The continuance of the pensions to Sylvester and Drayton is recommended in a note at the end of the account.

August 26, 1608. To one who presented two
bookes to his highnes . . . . 1 li.10 s.
October 10, 1608. To Mr. Browne [1] for a booke
given to his highnes . . . . 5 li.
October 25, 1608. To a poor scholer with a booke to
his highnes . . . . 3 li.
December 28, 1608. To Mr. Silvester yearlie be his
highnes comand . . . . 20 li.
January 3, 1608 (09). To Mr. Daniell [2] be comand 7 li.
January 5, 1608 (09). To one Mr. Cotton . . .
January 11, 1608 (09). To Mr. Hall's [3] man with a 10 li.
booke to his highnes . . . . 1 li.
January 16, 1608 (09). To the Schoolmaster of
Sant Martins who presented the Kings book in
emblems and pictures, to his highnes . . . 5 li.
February 1, 1608 (09). For the great Spanish bible
at his highnes command . . . . 20 li.
February 2, 1608 (09). To Sir Thomas Pavies man
with bookes to his highnes . . . . . 1 li. 10 s.
April 27, 1609. To a Duchman [4] that presented a
book of the law dedicated to his highnes . . . 5 li.
June 14, 1609. To Daniell the Italian by command 1 li. 10 s.
July 7, 1609. To the Bishop of Chichesters [5] man
with a booke to his highnes . . . . . . 1 li.

---

[1] This could hardly have been William Browne the poet, who, according to the accepted date of his birth, was at this time not over eighteen. The first part of his *Britannia's Pastorals*, however, seems to have been written before he was twenty. His elegy on the death of Henry was published, with another by Christopher Brooke, in 1613.

[2] Cf. p. lxxv.

[3] Joseph Hall, Dean of Gloucester (1617) and Bishop of Exeter (1627), was Henry's favorite chaplain. His *Epistles* (1608) were dedicated to the Prince, and contain letters to Chaloner, Newton, and Murray. His *Characters of Vertues and Vices*, dedicated to Lords Denny and Hay, appeared in the same year.

[4] Paul Buys's (Busius) commentary on the *Pandects* was dedicated to the Prince and sent to him with a letter dated April 11, 1609. (Birch, *Life of Henry*, p. 158.)

[5] Launcelot Andrewes. His *Tortura torti: sive; Ad Matthæi Torti Librum Responsio*, in answer to Cardinal Bellarmine's attack on James's *Apologie*, appeared in this year.

July 23, 1609. To Mr. Cheek for a booke of Emblems [1] . . . . 3 li.

Of the gifts and pensions bestowed in the years 1610–1612
the only one which appears in this earlier record is Sylvester's, the payment of which indicates that it ran over
the year 1608. It is probable, however, that it was granted
still earlier, as a reward, perhaps, for the collected edition
of his translations from Du Bartas, which appeared in
1605–1607 with a remarkable apparatus of dedicatory
sonnets in English, French and Italian, a chorus of the
muses, and a series of cones, pillars, and other geometrical
forms of poetry in honor of the King.[2] After Henry's death,
Sylvester published his *Lachrimæ Lachrymarum* (1612),
entered in the Stationers' Register as "A Viall of household teares . . . by his highnes fyrst worst Poett and
pensioner,"[3] and containing in the third edition elegies by
Donne,[4] Sir W. Cornwallis, Joseph Hall, Sir Edw. Herbert,
Sir Henry Goodyer, Geo. Gerard, S. T. C. (Sir Thomas
Chaloner), Henry Burton (Clerk of the Closet), and other
members of a literary group which was composed in part of
gentlemen of the Prince's household. To the Princess

---

[1] This may have been a MS. copy of a book entitled *Anagrammata et
Chron-Anagrammata regia, nunc primum in hâc formâ in lucem emissa*, London, 1613. The author was William Cheeke, who took the degree of B.A.
from Oxford in 1595. (*D. N. B.*)

[2] The opening of his translation of the *Furies* has a characteristic reference
to the King's earlier version : —

> " . . . But yer we pass, our slender Bark
> Must here strike top-sails to a Princely Ark
> Which keeps these Straights : Hee hails us threatfully,
> Star-board our helm; come underneath his Lee.
> .   .   .   .
> Vouchsafe to togh us at your Royall Stern."

[3] *Arber's Transcripts*, Vol. III, p. 230.

[4] An earlier evidence of Donne's connection with this circle is given by the
verses he contributed to Coryat's *Crudities* (1611). Coryat had been in the
household and dedicated his volume to the Prince, who was in the joke of
the mock-laudatory poems, and insisted on their publication. Donne also
sent Prince Henry a copy of *The Pseudo-Martyr*, accompanied by a letter
which is still preserved (MSS. of Marquis of Bath, *Hist. MSS. Comm. Reports*, III, p. 196).

Elizabeth Sylvester later dedicated his *Little Bartas* (1614), and to Prince Charles *The Parliament of Vertues Royall* (1614–1615) and *Maiden's Blush* (1620). The dedicatory sonnet of the 1614–1615 poem ends with the following picturesque appeal : —

> "You you alone (Great Prince) with Pities Grace,
> Have held my Chin above the Waters brinke :
> Hold still, alas ! hold stronger or I sinke,
> Or haile me up into som safer place,
> Som Privie Groom, som Room within your doores
> That, as my Heart, my Harpe may all be yours."

Peacham's assertion that Sylvester received "little or no reward, either for his paines or dedications," [1] if true at all, can be true only of this later period ; the poet at least did not fail for lack of perseverance.

There is no reference to the poet George Chapman in either of the accounts, a fact which serves to illustrate the incompleteness of the data they furnish. In a letter of appeal written to the King in 1613, Chapman states that "serving above nine yeares the late Prince Henry in place of a sewer in ordinary," he had been "put from his place under Prince Charles." He adds that having "four years attended the late Prince, he was commanded to continue his Homer," the 1609 and 1611 editions of which are dedicated to Henry. Chapman's name should thus be joined to those of Coryat, Sylvester, Owen, Lydyat, Hall, Drayton, and Daniel in the list of unequal but not unrepresentative Jacobean men of letters who were under the Prince's patronage. [2]

THE COURT OF QUEEN ANNE

For the patronage of the Queen, evidence similar to that in Murray's records is supplied by a document with the heading, *Accounts of the Queen's Household April–Jan.*

---

[1] *Truth of our Times*, 1638 (Sylvester's *Poems*, ed. Grosart, Introd., p. xix).   [2] *Athenæum*, April, 1901, p. 433.

1615 [*16*], the only one with details of this kind which the writer has found among the household accounts of James and Anne. Though it covers a period of less than a year, this gives a good idea of the character of the Queen's expenditures and the nature of her tastes. It is clear that she took especial pleasure in small charities, and her devotion to music is shown not only by the large yearly wages of the members of her French orchestra, but by daily gifts to strolling singers and musicians of every description. The following are the only items of literary significance: —

Baltassar Nardi,[1] Italian poett for so much paid and given unto him by warrant signed by her highnes dated at Greenw^ch the xxiii^th of November 1615 . . . . . xxx li.

Ellis Worth, one of her Ma^te plaiers for so much paid unto him in the behalfe of himselfe and the rest of his fellowes of that companie for one plaie acted before her Matie Queenes Court the xvii^th of December 1615. By warrant . . . vii^th of Januarie, 1615 [2] . . . . x li.

John Heminge one of the Kinge Ma^te plaiers for as much paid unto him in the behalfe of himselfe and the rest of his fellowes of that companie for one plaie acted before her Matie at Queenes Court on St Thomas daye at night being the xxi^th of December 1615. By warrant . . . xxii^th of Januarie 1615 [16] . . . . x li.

John Florio [3] one of the groomes of the Privie Chamber to her Matie for so much paid unto him and allowed for money by him disbursed for diverse necessaries for her Matie [Nov. 1, 1614 — Nov. 1, 1615, in all] . . . . vii li. v s.

---

[1] Nardi was a theologian as well as poet, and author of a defense of Roman supremacy, *Expunctiones locorum falsorum de papatu romano*, Paris, 1616, in refutation of the writings of Marcantonio de Dominis, Bishop of Spalato (Tiraboschi, *Storia della Letteratura Italiana*, 1780, p. 79). The latter was also in England, and was rewarded for his desertion of the Roman church by the Deanery of Windsor (*Docquets*, June, 1619) and the Mastership of the Savoy. The patronage extended to the two writers illustrates the divergence between the Queen and King in matters of religion.

[2] Neither this nor the following performance is recorded in the lists of Fleay or Murray (*English Dramatic Companies*).

[3] After the Queen's death Florio was granted a pension of £100 (*Cal. S. P. Dom.* January 21, 1620).

John Florio Groome of the privie chamber to her Matie
for his Annuitie or pension at c li. and for one whole yeare
ended at Michmas 1615 aforesaid and here allowed and
paid by virtue of her Maties l'res patente hereof to him made
dated at Whitehall the vth of August Anno sixo Re. Ja-
cobi . . . . c li.

Samuell Daniell Groome of the said privie chamber to her
Matie as well for his wages at xiii li. vi s. viii d. p. anno as
for his liverie at vi li. xiii s. iiii d. p. anno due for one whole
yeare ended at Michas 1615 aforesaid, wth xl li. of increase
and here allowed and paid as well according to the orders
and directions before mentioned as also by a warrant signed
by her highnes and dated the day of [blank] . . . lx li.

Sir Robert Aiton knight her Ma^{te} Secretarie and Maister
of Requeste for his wages at c li. p. anno for one whole yeare
ended at Michmas 1615 . . . . c li.

Aytoun, who had written Latin verses on the King's
accession, and carried the *Premonition* abroad in 1609, was
the successor of Sir William Fowler as the Queen's secretary.
He held the post from October 20, 1612,[1] until the Queen's
death, and afterward received a pension of £500[2] and under
Charles the same position in the household of Henrietta
Maria.

The service of the poet Daniel under Queen Anne was of
longer duration, extending from the time of her arrival in
England until her death. His name first appears in this
connection in a license, dated January 31, 1604, to Edward
Kirkham and others to train up a company "to be called
Children of the Revelle to the Queen," in which it is stipu-
lated that no plays be "presented by them before the Queen
or publicly acted but by the allowance of Samuell Daniel,
whom her Maties pleasure is to appoint for that purpose."[3]
As early as 1607 he was in possession of his place as a groom

---

[1] *Deputy Keeper's Reports*, II, p. 79.
[2] " . . . in consideration of his service to his Matie and the late Queen
Anne." — *Docquets* (*Cal. S. P. Dom.*, July, 1620).
[3] Devon, *Issues of the Exchequer in the Reign of James I*, 1836.

of the Queen's chamber, with the annual fee of £60. Among his pieces written for the Queen are the masque entitled *The Vision of the Twelve Goddesses*, presented January 8, 1603; *The Queen's Arcadia*, presented at Oxford, August 30, 1605, before the King and Queen; *Tethys Festival*, June 5, 1610; and *Hymen's Triumph*, February 3, 1614, before the King by the Queen's Court at the marriage of Lord Roxburghe. In the *Accounts*, Daniel is the only groom with an increase in addition to his regular wage, and almost the only one who receives no reimbursement for payments made in behalf of his mistress. Apparently, therefore, his position was nominal and did not require constant attendance. It is significant that his name appears, as it is here given, just after that of his friend Florio.

At this point it is necessary to return to two items in Murray's accounts of the Prince's household, one January 3, 1609, "To Mr. Daniell . . . 7 li.," and the other June 14, 1609, "To Daniell the Italian . . . 1 li. 10 s." The first of these undoubtedly refers either to the poet or to his brother, John Daniel, the musician, who was later master of the Queen's choir boys of Bristol.[1] The second might be passed over as insignificant, especially since there are numerous similar payments to poor scholars, artists of all kinds and degrees, and in one case to "an Italian jugler," were there not other evidence of considerable weight to connect it with the poet.

In the first place, there is his close friendship with the Italian language-master John Florio. Two of his sonnets written for Florio's works are addressed "To my deare friend . . ." and a third "To my deare friend and brother. . . ." Florio, it will be recalled, was the son of a Florentine Protestant who came to England shortly before the reign of Edward VI. The term "brother" no doubt refers merely to their fellowship in the Queen's service; but it seems likely that the poet helped Florio into this service, and that

---

[1] "A license unto John Daniel to form a company of children to be called The Children of her Ma^tle Royall Chamber of Bristol. . . ." — *Docquets*, June, 1615. Another license was granted to Daniel and others in May, 1622.

their friendship was the result of family intimacy and common race.

Other of Daniel's friends were Italians. In Wright's *Elizabeth and her Times* (Vol. II, p. 315), we hear of a Samuel Daniel abroad and in the company of an Italian doctor, Julio Marino. His *Description of Beauty translated out of Marino* can hardly be connected with the doctor, since the poet's given name was Giambattista, but it serves to illustrate Daniel's knowledge of Italian and interest in Italian literature. That he travelled in Italy in his youth is shown by the headings of two sonnets in the *Delia* sequence, "At the Author's going into Italie" (sonnet LII), and "This Sonnet was made at the Author's beeing in Italie" (sonnet LI). His first published work, entitled *Imprese*, was a translation of a Latin tract on crests and seals by the contemporary Italian historian, Paulus Jovius. His friendship with the poet Guarini is indicated by the following sonnet addressed to Sir Edward Dimmock, Daniel's first patron, on an English translation of Guarini's *Il Pastor Fido:* —

" I do rejoyce learned and worthy Knight,
    That by the hand of thy kinde Country-man
    (This painfull and industrious Gentleman)
    Thy deare esteem'd Guarini comes to light;
    Who in thy love I know tooke great delight
    As thou in his, who now in English can
    Speake as good English as Italian,
    And here enjoyes the grace of his owne right.
    Though I remember he hath oft imbas'd
    Unto us both the vertues of the North,
    Saying our costes were with no measures grac'd,
    Nor barbarous tongues could any verse bring forth.
    I would he sawe his owne, or knew our store,
    Whose spirits can yield as much, and if not more." [1]

Lines 9–12 of the sonnet refer clearly to conversation with Guarini, and apparently to a personal friendship. Fur-

[1] *Works*, ed. Grosart, Vol. I, p. 263.

thermore, though "our costes" in line 11 means England, it seems very unlikely that "*thy* kinde Country-man" in the second line would have been written by one who had every reason to consider the English translator quite as much his own countryman as Dimmock's.

Sidney or a dozen other Elizabethans might be proved Italians by such evidence as this. But it should be remembered that Daniel's brother and perhaps his father were musicians in an age when most musicians were foreigners; Ferrebosco, Bassano, Lupo, and others were all Italians. The name Daniel, or Daniell, should cause no difficulty, since it was borne by the Italian mentioned in the payment, and since it differs but slightly from the Italian forms Daniele, Danielli, or Daniello.

In short, the value of the evidence depends on its cumulative effect. We have a payment to an Italian named Daniel from the same source and not long after a payment to the poet; we know that the latter came of a family of musicians, that he traveled in Italy, translated from Italian writers, spoke the language, and had as his best friend a man of the same stock. In the absence of exact information regarding his birth and parentage, these seem sufficient reasons for assuming that the stylistic purity of "well-languaged" Daniel was that of a writer for whom English was not strictly the mother tongue.

If this be true, it may help to explain the statement of a German traveler in England in 1615 that the Queen's household, with the exception of the secretary and comptroller, was largely French and Italian.[1] The motive for such a choice of servants would be her half open acceptance of the Catholic faith. Daniel himself, according to Wood, was "in animo catholicus."

THE COURT OF KING JAMES

During his reign in England, as has already been pointed out, James took no very active interest in poetry, being

---

[1] *Zur Geschichte Jacob I*, Oppelin, 1857, p. 15.

content, apparently, that his reputation should rest on the accomplishments of his greener years. He and Alexander still at times pottered with the psalms, but, aside from these, only two or three fragments of his verse are of a later date than 1603. Even the collection of poems now printed, though perhaps intended for publication at the same time as the folio volume of his prose, does not seem to have been generally known during his life.

Obviously, therefore, whatever influence the King may have had on the trend of English poetry was not by direct example, but by the effect of his personal likes and dislikes on the taste of the court and on the work of writers whose verse was intended partly to meet his approval. It would of course be absurd to attribute to any single influence, and in particular to an influence so limited as that of the King, fashions so widespread as those of the so-called "metaphysical school," which prevailed during his reign; and, as will appear, though his verse and prose have some of the defects of this school, his later views were distinctly opposed to its subtlety of thought and rough obscurity of style. But on the other hand, the opposite tendency, toward more familiar themes and a more conventional treatment of metre and diction, shown especially in a preference for the closed and regular or 'classical' pentameter couplet, developed chiefly among a group of court poets, who catered to a small body of courtly readers and who would have special reason to make their verse conform to the tastes of royalty. *A priori*, at least, there is nothing unreasonable in the postulate that in the reign of James, as in France during the same period [1] and later in England during the Restoration, the taste of King and court had a definite and marked influence on contemporary literature.

Among English poets who sought court favor, Ben Jonson's way was made easy by his Scottish extraction, scholar-

---

[1] "L'ordre et la discipline, l'exacte probité que le roi s'efforçait d'introduire dans les affaires et dans les mœurs, Malherbe eut comme la mission de les faire, lui, introduire pour le premier fois dans l'empire du caprice même, et de la fantasie (Brunetière, "La Reforme de Malherbe," *Revue des Deux Mondes*, December 1, 1892).

ship, and a bluff joviality of disposition, not by any means above gross flattery. His five years spent in the household of d'Aubigny, the King's cousin, may be considered a sign of this favor, as well as the pension of one hundred marks (£100 after 1630) and the tierce of canary which he received from 1616 until his death. The story that the King would have knighted the poet, had the latter been willing,[1] has every mark of probability in its favor. Jonson's duties as deviser of masques must have required frequent attendance at court and on royal progresses; and if the King retained as lively an interest in these entertainments as he had formerly shown in Scotland, he would have been eager to discuss and plan them with his poet laureate.

Casual remarks of the latter recorded in Drummond's *Conversations* suggest such intercourse, though no great respect on the part of the poet for the opinions of his sovereign. On one occasion, according to Jonson, the King expressed the view that "Sir P. Sidney was no poet. Neither did he see ever any verses in England equal to the scullor's [Taylor the Water Poet]." [2] The natural inference from this is that James was no critic, but it may well be rather that the remark was not intended seriously or that Jonson was a malicious reporter. There is abundant evidence that Sidney was the one English poet of the preceding generation to whom the King felt free to pay tribute. Spenser's treatment of Mary and her son in *The Faërie Queene* made him impossible, and who else was there to set over against Ronsard and Du Bartas and the long line of Italian poets? According to Henry Leigh's report of an interview with James, September, 1599, the latter "comended Sir Philip Sydney for the best and swetest wryter that ever he knewe — surely it seemeth he loved him muche." [3] It is noteworthy in this connection that Drummond pronounced Spenser's *Amoretti* "childish," but con-

---

[1] Jonson's *Works*, ed. Cunningham, Introd., p. cxx.
[2] *Ibid.*, Vol. IX, p. 398.
[3] *Calendar of Border Papers*, Vol. II, p. 649. Cf. also James's epitaph on Sidney (XXX), and note. The second edition of the *Arcadia* was published in Edinburgh in 1599.

sidered Sidney's *Arcadia* "the most excellent work that, in my Judgement, hath been written in any language that I understand." [1]

On another occasion, Ben told the King plainly that " his master, M. G. Buchanan, had corrupted his eare when young, and learned him to sing verses when he should have read them." [2] One may infer that there had been a discussion of the old question as to whether verse stands by metre or sense, in which the King's position was not so ill-taken as in his remarks on English writers. One of Jonson's epigrams, *To King James* (No. IV), plays on the familiar theme of his excellence as prince and poet : —

"How, best of kings, dost thou a scepter bear?
How, best of poets, dost thou laurel wear?
But two things rare the Fates had in their store,
And gave thee both, to show they could no more.
For such a poet, while thy days were green,
Thou wert, as chief of them are said t' have been.
And such a prince thou art, we daily see,
As chief of those still promise they will be.
Whom should my muse then fly to, but the best
Of kings, for grace; of poets, for my test."

Tribute of this sort may be discounted; but it is more significant that the copy of the *Poeticall Exercises at vacant houres* which Gillies used in preparing his reprint contained the inscription, —

"Tanquam Explorator.
BEN. JONSON."

— and numerous corrections of spelling in the handwriting of the poet.[3] "I am arrived safely," wrote Jonson to Drummond (May 10, 1619) on his return from Scotland, "with a most Catholick Welcome, and my Reports not unacceptable to His Majesty: He professed (I thank God) some Joy to

---

[1] *Works*, ed. 1711, p. 161. For his borrowings from Sidney, cf. Kastner, *Modern Language Review*, January, 1911.

[2] Jonson's *Works*, Vol. IX, p. 407.   [3] Gillies, *Preface*, p. xviii.

see me, and is pleased to hear of the Purpose of my Book." [1]
This last was no doubt the

". . . journey into Scotland sung,
With all the adventures, [2]

— which was destroyed by fire with other of his manuscripts.
On Drummond's verses his critic in the *Conversations* passed
the general censure that "They were all good, especially
my 'Epitaph of the Prince,' save that they smelled too
much of the schools . . . yett that he wished for pleasing
the King, that Piece of *Forth Feasting* had been his own." [3]
The last remark has a twofold significance, since while it
illustrates, with the ones preceding, the regard attached to
the good opinion of the King, it suggests also the kind of
poem which might be expected to win it. *Forth Feasting*,
written for the King's return to Edinburgh, is not more
grossly flattering than a hundred others, and is a model of
smoothly flowing, neatly confined couplets.

Flattery somewhat more subtle than Jonson's, and additional evidence that the King's verse and criticism had
some circulation in England, is contained in a poem by Sir
John Beaumont, consisting of sixty-six carefully polished
lines *To his late Maiesty, concerning the True Forme of English Poetry.* [4] The piece need not be considered insincere,
since the views expressed are in accord with the author's
practice in his early and later verse, but it is clear, nevertheless, that he had just been reading the *Reulis and cautelis*,
and sought to echo in his tribute the opinions there set
forth. His source is referred to in the tenth line, —

"When your judicious rules have been my guide,"

— and is evident enough in his vague allusions to "colors"
and "flowing," with which in the sense of rhyme and metre

---

[1] Drummond's *Works*, ed. 1711, p. 154.
[2] *An Execration upon Vulcan*, ll. 98–99.
[3] Drummond, p. 226.
[4] *Poems*, ed. Grosart, p. 118. The piece was of course written before the
King's death, the title being added in the first edition of 1629.

he was perhaps unfamiliar. The following are the more important parallels : —

R. and C., Chap. I. "That you "keip just cullouris"; *i.e.* avoid rhyming with the same word, rhyme on the accented syllable and from there to the end, and avoid rhymes of three or even two syllables, the last of which are "eatin in the pronounceing." Beaumont repeats this idea, but appears uncertain about the meaning of the word "cullouris" : —

> "Vouchsafe to be our Master, and to teach
>   Your English poets to direct their lines,
>   To mixe their colours, and expresse their signes."
> —ll. 4–6.

> "Our Saxon shortness hath peculiar grace,
>   In choice of words, fit for the ending place,
>
>   .   .   .   .
>
>   These must not be with disproportion lame,
>   Nor should an eccho still repeate the same."
> —ll. 39–44.

Chap. II. That you keep "the flowing"; *i.e.* avoid variant feet and other irregularities. This must have suggested : —

> " When verses like a milky torrent flow,
>   They equall temper in the poet show."
> —ll. 13–14.

> "On halting feet the ragged poem goes
>   With accents, neither fitting verse nor prose."
> —ll. 23–24.

Chap. III. Avoid padding, and "frame your wordis and sentencis according to the mater." A passage of similar import occurs in the *Basilikon Doron*, where the Prince is warned against "book-language and pen and ink-horn

termis, and least of all mignard and effeminate termis."
Further: "If ye would write worthily choose subjects
worthy of you, that be not full of vanity but of virtue,
eschewing obscurity, and delighting ever to be plain and
sensible. And if ye writis in Verse, remember that it is not
the principal part of a poem to rime right and flow well
with many pretty wordis, but the chief commendation of a
poem is, that when the verse shall be shaken sundrie in
prose, it shall be found so rich in quicke inventions, and
poetick flowers, and in faire and pertinent comparisons, as
it shall retaine the lustre of a Poem, although in prose."
Compare with this the following lines from Beaumont: —

   'Pure phrase, fit epithet, a sober care
    Of metaphors, descriptions cleare, yet rare,
    Similitudes contracted smooth and round,
    Not vext by learning, but with nature crown'd."
                                — ll. 51-54.

  "To easie use of that peculiar gift,
    Which poets in their raptures hold most deare,
    When actions by their lively sound appeare."
                                — ll. 60-62

  "For though in termes of art their skill they close,
    And joy in darksome words as well as those:
    They yet have perfect sense more pure and cleare
    Than envious Muses, which sad garlands weare
    Of dusky clouds, their strange conceits to hide."
                                — ll. 27-31.

After the third chapter, James has four shorter ones on
comparisons and ornaments, and ends with an interesting
list of "the kyndis of versis." It is notable that while he
condemns the pentameter couplet as "ryme quhilk servis
onely for lang histories, and yet are nocht verse," Beaumont
considers it the best of metres and in his published verse
uses it almost exclusively : —

"The relish of the Muse consists in rime,
  One verse must meete another like a chime.

  .   .   .   .

  In many changes these may be exprest:
  But those that joyne most simply, run the best."
                                        — ll. 37-49.

In his practice, the poet conforms to these conservative
precepts by the avoidance of the metrical irregularities and
to a lesser extent of the conceitfulness of his fellow-poets.
"No one, indeed," says Mr. Gosse, "was in 1602 writing
the heroic couplet so 'correctly' as the author of the *Metamorphosis [of Tabacco]*."[1] This early piece was published
anonymously, but there is little doubt of Beaumont's
authorship.

It has, I think, not been pointed out that his historical
poem entitled *Bosworth Field*, his lost *Crown of Thorns*,[2] all
of his so-called "Royal and Courtly Poems," in short, the
greater number of the pieces gathered together in the first
(posthumous) edition of 1629, were written much later, during the closing years of James's reign, when the good will
of his kinsman George Villiers, Duke of Buckingham, drew
him out of his long retirement and led him to seek favor
at court with his pen: —

  "My Muse, which tooke from you her life and light
  Sate like a weary wretch, whome suddaine night

[1] *The Jacobean Poets*, p. 107.
[2] This was dedicated to the Earl of Southampton, who was released from
imprisonment in 1621 and died in 1624. Cf. Beaumont's *Elegy:* —

> "He is a father to my crowne of thornes :
>   Now since his death how can I ever look,
>   Without some teares, upon that orphan booke?"

The suggestion may be ventured that the poem had some connection with
the King's *Meditation* on Matthew xxvii. 27–29, with sub-title *A paterne
for a Kings inauguration* (1620), a lengthy sermon and application of the
narrative of Christ's coronation by Pilate. A monarch, writes James,
"must not expect a soft and easie croune, but a croune full of thornie cares
yea of platted and intricate cares. . . ."

Had overspred : your absence casting downe
The flow'rs and Sirens' feathers from her crowne;
Your favour first th' anointed head inclines
To heare my rurall songs and reade my lines :
Your voyce, my reede with lofty musick reares
To offer trembling songs to princely eares." [1]

Buckingham's mother (created Countess of Buckingham in 1618) was of the Beaumonts of Cole-Orton, and thus connected with the family of the poet. The latter, though Grosart speaks of his Puritanism, was in point of fact a Catholic,[2] and it is likely, therefore, that his retirement on his estate at Gracedieu did not end much before 1618, when the whole court veered toward catholicism in view of the approaching Spanish marriage. In February, 1617, Buckingham's mother changed her faith, and became, according to Wilson, "the cynosure that all the Papists steered by."

Beaumont's poems in these years were all of the courtly and occasional character which Waller later made popular, on such themes as the twentieth anniversary of James's reign (1623), his deliverance from a dangerous accident (January 8, 1622), his glorious memory, the Prince's journey and return, his marriage, etc. *Bosworth Field* is of the same period, since a dozen or more lines are devoted to praise of James and "hopefull Charles," —

". . . born t'asswage
The winds that would disturb this golden age."

Of the favorable reception of these poems there can be little question. *My Lord of Buckingham's Welcome to the King at Burley*, written by Beaumont, was answered in verse by the King (App. II, VI, VII), and these in turn called forth Beaumont's sonnet *Of his Majestie's Vow for the Felicity of My Lord Marquesse of Buckingham*, in which,

---

[1] *To the Duke of Buckingham on his Return from Spain* (1622).

[2] Cf. *Cal. S. P. Dom.*, November 14, 1607: "Gift . . . of the late dissolved monastery of Grace Dieu, and other lands in Leicester, in the hands of the Crown by the recusancy of John Beaumont."

as in those of James, there are only five rhymes. The dates of his poems and the circumstances in which they were written are of considerable importance in connection with his claims as one of the early polishers of the couplet.

Whether Waller was at court in these years his biographers do not make clear; but it is thought that he sat, as a youth of sixteen, in the parliament of 1621, and it was at the close of either this parliament or that of 1624 that he went "either out of curiosity or respect, to see the King at dinner, with whom were Dr. Andrews, Bishop of Winchester, and Dr. Neal, Bishop of Durham, standing behind his Majesty's chair." His verses *Of the Danger his Majesty (being Prince) Escaped in the Road at Saint Andrews* refer to an event which occurred in 1623, but allusions to the French marriage make it possible that the poem was not written before 1625. It was at least not later than this year that he began his series of occasional pieces, addressed to royalty, on themes of current and courtly interest, and in a style which in the next generation was to gain general acceptance. This handsome, pliant-tempered, "brisk young spark" of twenty was scarcely the one to create a new fashion in poetry, though he would be among the first to adapt his muse to a manner which had received the proper sanction. It is doubtful, therefore, if one need seek even so far as the stanzas of Fairfax's *Tasso* for the models which guided him in his earliest verse.[1]

Aside from Jonson and Beaumont, the men of literary accomplishments who were in the King's immediate circle were for the most part Scotchmen, long in the service of the King, and with tastes and training similar to his own. To this group belong several members of the Murray family: Sir David, Prince Henry's master of the robes; Sir Thomas, tutor and secretary to Charles, and the predecessor of Wotton as Provost of Eton; John Murray, a gentleman of

[1] It is noteworthy that Fairfax also was given royal approval. James is said to have valued his *Tasso* above all other poetry (Jonson, *Works*, ed. Cunningham, Vol. IX, p. 366). The second edition of Fairfax (1624), which probably attracted Waller's attention, was printed at the command of James, and was dedicated to Prince Charles.

the King's privy chamber; and Sir Patrick Murray, also a member of the royal household. Their verse which has survived is of little interest, chiefly dedicatory sonnets and pieces in Latin, but Byron's line, —

"And 'tis some praise in peers to write at all,"

— may be applied to courtiers of every rank. On the death of John Murray, April 17, 1615, Sir William Alexander was stirred to sing of him in terms of high praise: —

"Mourn Muses, mourn, your greatest Gallant dies,
Who still in State did court your sacred Train;
Your Minion Murray, Albion's sweetest Swain."

The King commended these lines, but thought they gave Murray too much praise.[1]

Sir Robert Ker, remembered chiefly for his friendship with Donne and Jonson, was another of the King's familiars. In one of his letters to Drummond is *A Sonnet in praise of a Solitary Life*, written from "the very Bed-chamber, where I could not sleep"[2] — presumably the king's chamber, since he was at this time one of his regular attendants. Another letter, April, 1624, is accompanied by ten verse paraphrases of the Psalms.[3]

These may have been written in connection with the paraphrase over which James occupied his spare moments before and after his coming to England. His chief collaborator, however, was Sir William Alexander (1567?–1646), who was created Earl of Stirling in 1633. Alexander began his career at Court as tutor and afterward gentleman of the chamber to Prince Henry. In 1614 he was appointed master of requests, and rose to high rank and responsibility in the courts of James and Charles. The correspondence which he kept up after 1614 with the poet Drummond in Scotland contains frequent references to his association with James in literary exercises. "I received your last Letter," he writes, April 18, 1620, "with the Psalm you sent,

[1] Drummond's *Works*, ed. 1711, p. 151.
[2] *Ibid.*, p. 153.   [3] *Arch. Scot.*, Vol. IV, p. 93.

which I think very well done; I had done the same, long before it came, but he [James] prefers his own to all else, tho' perchance, when you see it, you will think it the worst of the Three. No man must meddle with that Subject, and therefore I advise you to take no more Pains therein."[1] Opinions so frank as this Alexander probably did not express in the presence of majesty.

The paraphrase on which they were engaged seems to have been intended by James as a supplement to the King James version of the Bible — an undertaking which (it may be noted) he had broached before the General Assembly at Burntisland as early as 1601. On coming to England, according to Spottiswoode, he "set the most learned divines of that church a-work for the translation of the Bible . . . but the revising of the Psalms he made his own labour, and . . . went through a number of them, commending the rest to a faithful and learned servant, who hath therein answered his M. expectation."[2]

Having obtained a privilege from Charles in 1627, Alexander published in that year and reissued in 1631 what purported to be King James's paraphrase, and another entirely different version in 1636.[3] Neither of these is at all like the MS. paraphrase in the British Museum, which contains rough drafts in the King's hand (with fair copies in some cases) of Psalms 1–7, 9–21, 29, 47, 100, 125, 128, 133, 148, 150, Eccles. xii, the Lord's Prayer (cf. App. II, IX) and Deut. xxxii. The initials J. D. R. S. (Jacobus Dominus Rex Scotia?), frequently signed to the rough drafts, indicate that they were made before the King left Scotland. It is not impossible, therefore, that Alexander's first edition was based on a later paraphrase in which he and James collaborated; the royal recommendation opposite the title-page of the 1631 edition testifies explicitly to James's authorship.

[1] Drummond's *Works*, p. 151.

[2] *History of the Church of Scotland*, ed. 1847, Vol. III, p. 99.

[3] Bound up in 1637 with *The Book of Common Prayer . . . for the Use of the Church of Scotland*. The attempt to enforce the use of this service caused the Edinburgh Presbyterian Riot of July 23, 1637.

Another of Alexander's letters, dated February 4, 1616, contains the King's sonnet *Against the Could that was in January 1616*, and his own verses suggested by it. The letter deals also with a literary discussion in which they had engaged: "The last Day being private with his Majesty, after other Things, we fortuned to discourse of *English* Poesy, and I told one Rule that he did like of exceedingly, which was this; *That, to make a good Sound there must still be first a short Syllable, and then a long, which is not positively long of itself, but comparatively, when it followeth a shorter; so that one Syllable may be long in one Place and short in another, according as it is matched; for a Syllable seems short when it is as it were born down with a longer.*" [1]

With this comment on a point of prosody may be joined James's sonnet (XLVI) on *Sir William Alexander's Harshe Verses after the Ingliche Fasone*, the clearest expression of his distaste for the rough obscurity of the metaphysical poets: —

"... Although your neighbours have conspir'd to spill
That art which did the Laurel crowne obtaine
And borrowing from the raven there ragged quill
Bewray there harsh, hard trotting tumbling wayne
 Such hamringe hard the metalls hard require
 Our songs are fil'd with smoothly flowing fire."

This may have no definite reference, but it is in keeping with James's views elsewhere disclosed, and would be an appropriate condemnation of the unconventionality affected by Donne and his followers. In a letter to Arthur Johnston, one of the royal physicians, Drummond voices still more explicitly the views of the older school. The letter is undated, but Johnston was physician to James for some time before the latter's death. The writer speaks first of the eminence and permanence of poetry. "In vain," he continues, "have some Men of late, (Transformers of

---

[1] Drummond's *Works*, p. 149. For the first part of the letter, cf. XLVII, note.

every Thing) consulted upon her reformation, and endeavoured to abstract her to Metaphysical Idea's, and Scholastical Quiddities, denuding her of her own Habits, and those Ornaments with which she hath amused the World some Thousand Years. *Poesy* is not a Thing that is yet in the finding and search, or which may be otherwise found out, being already condescended upon by all Nations, and as it were established *jure Gentium*, amongst *Greeks*, *Romans*, *Italians*, *French*, *Spaniards*. Neither do I think that a good Piece of *Poesy*, which *Homer*, *Virgil*, *Ovid*, *Petrarch*, *Bartas*, *Ronsard*, *Boscan*, *Garcilasso*, (if they were alive, and had that Language) could not understand, and reach the Sense of the Writer. . . . What is not like the Ancients and conform to those Rules which hath been agreed unto by all Times, may (indeed) be something like unto *Poesy*, but it is no more *Poesy* than a Monster is a Man." [1]   This is probably the first use of the term *metaphysical* in connection with the group of poets to which it was afterward applied by Dryden, Pope, and Dr. Johnson. While the passage consists of traditional classical formulæ, these for the writer were by no means dead or empty; and they express the attitude of himself and his friends as clearly as they anticipate the view of poetry which was to prevail during the next hundred and fifty years.

Though not in the court, Drummond was in close touch with it, and would voice its tastes so far as these were determined by the King and his household intimates. The verse of these writers, it is true, was in many ways different from that of Waller and the later school, especially in the absence of stereotyped epithet, smart antithesis, and a general air of urbanity. But conservatism is not innovation, and so far as the correctness of the later poets was a return to accepted tradition, it found sanction in the theory and practice of the court poets of the reign of James. Drummond, Jonson, and George Sandys have usually been considered as the immediate precursors of Waller, especially in the use of the confined or classical heroic couplet.

[1] *Ibid.*, p. 143.

Sandys, it will be remembered, was a gentleman of the chamber to Charles, and wrote a part of his translation of Ovid's *Metamorphoses* in the early twenties of the century. Waller also was about the court when the opposition to the school of conceits was gathering head.

All of this evidence is intended chiefly to support two conclusions: (1) that during James's reign there was a well-defined sentiment at court in favor of a smooth, clear style in poetry (and also in prose); (2) that the writers who anticipated the manner and matter of later classicism came directly under this influence. It need not be assumed that James himself was in any large way responsible for these changes, save as an instrument or as one who adopted and spread abroad the theories he had been trained to accept. But his place made his views very influential, while his natural gifts were not contemptible; and there is little in the so-called innovations of Waller which could not have been derived from the formal views of poetry held by the King, and put in practice, partly on this account, but chiefly through personal preference, by the poets with whom he was associated.

AMATORIA

[I]

From sacred throne in heaven Empyrick hie
A breathe divine in Poëts brests does blowe
Wherethrough all things inferiour in degrie
As vassalls unto them doe hommage showe
There songs enchants Apollos selfe ye knowe   5
And chaste Dianas coache can haste or staye
Can change the course of Planets high or lowe
And make the earthe obeye them everie waye
Make rockes to danse, huge hills to skippe and playe
Beasts, foules, and fishe to followe them allwhere   10
Though thus the heaven, the sea, and earthe obeye,
Yett mutins the midde region of the aire,
    What hatefull Juno, Æolus entiseth
    Wherby contrarious Zephyre thus ariseth.

[II]

O cruell Cupide what a rutheles rage
What hatefull wrathe thou utterest upon me
No medicine my sicknesse may asswage
Nor cataplasme cure my wounde I see
Through deadlie shott alive I daylie dye   5
I frie in flammes of that envenomed darte
Which shotte me sicker in at [2] ather eye
Then fastned fast into my hoalit [3] harte
The fever hath infected everie parte
My bones are dried there marrowe melts awaye   10

---

[1] Title in the hand of Charles.   [2] Orig. *into.*
[3] Orig., *tormented;* crossed through and *hoalit* written above. Corrections in the MS. are usually made in this way.

My sinnowes feebles through my smoaking smarte
And all my bloode as in a pann doth playe
    I onlie wishe for ease of all my paine
    That she might witt what sorrowe I sustaine.

[III]

TO THE QUEENE [1]

  As on the wings of your enchanting fame
I was transported ou'r the stormie seas
Who coulde not quenche that restles burning flame
Which onlie ye by sympathie did mease
5 So can I troubled be with no disease
Bot ye my onlie Medicinar remaines
And easilie when ever that ye please
May salve my sores and mitigatt my paines
Your smiling is an antidote againes
10 The Melancholie that oppresseth me
And when a raging wrathe into me raignes
Your loving lookes may make me calme to be
    How oft you see me have an heavie hart
    Remember then sweete Doctour on your art.

[IV]

TO THE QUEENE, ANONIMOS [1]

  That blessed houre when first was brought to light
Our earthlie Juno, and our gratious Queene
Three Goddesses how soone they hade her seene
Contended who protect her shoulde by right
5 Bot being as Goddesses of equall might
And as of female sexe like stiffe in will
It was agreed by sacred Phœbus skill
To joyne there powers to blesse that blessed wight.

<hr>

[1] Titles in the hand of Carey.

Then happie Monarch sprung of Ferguse race
That talkes with wise Minerve when pleaseth the   10
And when thou list sume Princelie sporte to see
Thy chaste Diana rides with the in chase
    Then when to bed thou gladlie [1] does repaire
    Clasps in thine armes thy Cytherea faire.

[V]

TWO SONNETS TO HER M.^{TIE} TO SHOW THE DIFFERENCE
OF STILES [2]

Althogh [3] Madame I ought not to refuse
What yee request, or please [4] to desire
Yet may I justly make my own excuse
In that which last it pleas'd you to require
Long since forsooth my Muse beganne to tire   5
Through daylie fascherie of my own affaires
Which quench'd in me that heavenly furious fire
In place whereof came sad & thorny cares
Which restlesly no time nor season spares
To spoile me of my former pleasurs quite   10
Who wont before to use farre other wares
As exercis'd some worthy work to write
    How ar Castalias floods dried up in me
    Like suddain shoures this time of yeere ye see

[VI]

But what Madame & shall I then denie
Your juste demaunde and disobey the same?
No yee even yee shall carrie to the skie
My barren verse and shall my Muse inflame
Was it not only your inchaunting fame   5
Who on her wings alofte did carrie mee
Frome native soil to follow on your name

---

[1] Orig., *wearie*.
[2] This sonnet and the one following are in the handwriting of Charles.
[3] Orig., *suppose*.   [4] Orig., *pleaseth*.

And Eagle like on Theatis back to flee
Wher she commaunded Neptune for to be
10 My Princely guard and Triton to attend
On artificial flying ooars of tree
Wherin I resting ranne to journeys end
Then since your fame hath made me flie before
Well may your name my verses nou decore

[VII]

The Cheviott hills doe with my state agree
In everie point excepting onelie one
For as there toppes in cloudes are mounted hie
So all my thoughts in skies be higher gone
5 There foote is fast, my faithe a stedfast stone
From them discends the christall fontains cleare
And from mine eyes butt fained [1] force and mone
Hoppes trickling teares with sadd and murnefull cheare
From them great windes doe hurle with hiddeous beir
10 From me deepe sighs, greate flocks of sheepe they feede
I flockes of love, no fruicts on them appeare
My houpe to me no grace can bring or breede
In these alike, in this we disagree
That snowe on them, and flames remaines in me.

[VIII]

As man, a man am I composed all
Of brethren foure which did this worlde compone
Yett unto me doth suche a chance befall
As I of mankind all am he alone
5 Who of the foure possesseth onlie one
My flames of love to firie heaven be past
My aire in sighs evanish'd is and gone
My moysture into teares distilling fast
Now onelie earthe remaines with me at last
10 That am denuded of the other three

---

[1] Orig., *with fainted*. Altered by Carey.

Then crewell Dame since unto [1] suche a cast
Your onelie beautie thus compelleth me
   Send als [2] my earth, with earth for to remaine
   Or els restore me to my selfe againe.

[IX]

If he that lackes the light may justlie mone
And eke lament his miserable cace
As he to whome all worldlie joye is gone
When drearie darknes cumes in Phœbus place
How muche the more may I lament allace   5
The absence of my onelie lampe of light
Since Lezardlike I feede upon her face
And suckes my satisfaction from her sight
No more may I, then marigolde by night
Beare blossomes when no sighte [3] of sunne I have   10
For you Madame have by your beauties might
Bereft, and brookes my hart your humble slave
   How may a man, a floure, a corps in smart
   See, blossom, breathe; but eyes, but sunne, but hart.

[X]

Come [4] fruictfull thoughts that fertill ever flowes
And showes what sicknes smites my heavie hart
The more I muse my greefe the greater growes
And painefull pangues of passions playe there parte
My evill it is incurable by art   5
And keepis a contrare course to nature cleene
My minde delights to panse [5] upon his smart
And feede on flames though secrete and unseene
Bot as my brest a butt full long hath bene
To [6] sightles shotts, so on the other side   10
O ye my harts allurer by my eyen
Respect with ruthe the bale I daylie bide

[1] Orig., *into*.
[2] Orig., *this*.
[3] Orig., *light*.
[4] Orig., *Ouer*.
[5] *Muse* is written above in the hand of Charles, but crossed through and replaced by *panse* in the hand probably of James.
[6] Orig., *Of*.

Then since we bothe like sorrowe doe sustaine
Bothe preasse to turne in pleasure all our paine.

[XI]

Although that crooked crawling Vulcan lie
An-under ashes colde as oft we see
As senseless deade whill by his heate he drie
The greene and sizzing [1] faggots made of tree
5 Then will that little sponke and flaming eye
Bleaze bravelie forth and sparkling all abreed
With wandling up a wondrous sight to see
Kithe clearlie then and on the faggots feede
So am I forced for to confesse indeede
10 My sponke of love smor'd under coales of shame
By beauties force the fosterer of that seede
Now budds and bursts in an appearing flame
    Bot since your beautie hath this wonder wroght
    I houpe Madame it shall not be for noght.

[XII]

O womans witt that wavers with the winde
When none so well may warie now as I
As weathercocke thy stablenes I finde
And as the sea that still can never lie
5 Bot since that tyme the trueth hath made me trie
That in inconstance thou art constant still
My courage sayes on Cupide ceasse to crie
That are rewarded thus for thy goodwill
For thogh Madame I failde not to fullfill
10 All sort of service to a Mistres dewe
Yett absence thogh bot for a space did spill
The thankes deserved of all my service trewe
    What shall [2] I saye, I never thought to see
    That out of sight, shoulde out of langour be.

[1] Orig., *sissing.*   [2] Orig., *shoulde.*

[XIII]

CONSTANT LOVE IN ALL CONDITIONS

Now doeth disdainfull Saturne sadd and olde
With ycie bearde enjoye his frosen raigne
His hoarie haires and snowie mantle colde
Ou'rcovers hills and everie pleasant plaine
Whiles deaz'd with frost, whiles droun'd with rapping raine 5
Doe beasts and birds bewaile there carefull cace,
With longsume lookes in houpe to see againe
Sweete favoured Flora showe her aimeled face.

And looke how long they are in this estate,
This dolent season so there courage dants   10
That now no Cupide with his golden bate
Darr make there harts his harbour where he hants
Bot rather deade as are the trees and plants,
There spirits of life must hide them at the hart
Wherethrough there kindlie courage daylie scants   15
Whill mounting Phœbus makes them to revert.

And shall I then like birde or beast forgett
For anie stormes that threatning heaven can send
That object sweete, wheron my hart is sett
Whome for to serve my senses all I bend   20
My inward flame with colde it dothe contend
The more it burnes, the more restrain'd it be
No winters frost, nor sommers heate can end
Or staye the course of constant love in me.

[XIV]

A DIER AT HER M :^{TIES} DESYER : [1] —

If mourning might amend my harde unhappie cace
Or if complaining coulde appease Dame Fortunes frowning
    face

[1] Orig., *A Dier on her Matie*. The change in the title is made by Carey.
Printed in Rait, with the supplied title, *If Mourning micht Amende.*

Then shoulde I never cease by songs and sonnets still
With my to just conceaved regraits the earthe and aire to
fill
5 My cairfull cries and grones shoulde make the rockes re-
bounde
The mountains rive and all the earth with Echoes to re-
sounde
Not Orpheus [1] charming notes for his departed wife
Nor raging Roland for his love that ledd so madd a life
No not the world in one compared should never be
10 Unto the mone that I shoulde make, suche passions mar-
tyrs me
But what may [2] that availe except for to renewe
My olde and deeplie rooted griefs that els to gladly grewe
To rankle up the sore that lurkes into my hart
And as a cancer make it spreade abroade in everie part.
15 What wrathe have all the Gods conceaved at me allace
That makes me love where hatred dwells, and pittie hath
no place
O if she were bot faire, or if she were bot false
Bot faire and false torments me thus and holdes me by the
halse
If beautie as it ought with bountie coupled ware
20 Then suirlie she wolde pittie take on my consuming caire
Or if she wear but [3] false and lacking Venus grace
Then woulde I not have been abused by her enchanting face
Thus am I tortured still, I mourne without remeade
My languour lackes one [4] graine of houpe to mixe with daylie
dreade
25 My teares getts no regarde, my sighs can have no eare
And in one houre is quite forgott my service manie a yeare
What houpe can rest behinde, what may I looke for then
Bot be a butt to heavenlie plagues, a monstre amongs men
My state can never change my griefs are bot begunne
30 Thus casten is my luckles lott that woefull weirds have
spunne

---

[1] Orig., *with* deleted after *Orpheus.*
[2] Orig., Rait, *can.*
[3] Rait, *had bene.*
[4] Orig., Rait, *a.*

Awaye with comfort then and wellcome colde dispaire
And since I can have no delight, lett me delight in caire
My mirth in murning be, my joye in dolours deepe
I will with sadd and sorie sighs my selfe from languour keepe
And for my cheefest sports to mind then will I bring   35
As in a roll my whole mishaps, syne[1] like a swanne them
    sing
My houpe is whole transformed in blacke and colde dis-
    paire
Except I onlie houpe for deathe to end continuall caire :
No, death he must not haste, my mischiefs woulde he
    mend
It best becumes my miserie to dwine before I[2] end   40
Yett if the endles smart and sorrowe I sustaine
Were suffered for sume worthie wight, I happie wolde re-
    maine
I wolde me happie thinke if thus I martyred ware
For sume sweete Sainct in sacrifice that both were good and
    faire
Bot O allace my paine and restless griefe it growes   45
For her who never once on me a loving thought bestowes
Yett lett not this dishart no happie man in love
Who finds a maike that will not change, nor for no chance
    remove.
All wemen are in overs,[3] in vertue sume excell
And sume in vices may ou'rmatche the greatest Divell in 50
    hell
The blessedest creatures made by God the Angells ware
The cursedest creatures in the worlde the fallen Angells are
For me I onlie crave a spectacle to be
Wherin as in a masse confused all miseries men may see
And when my happ shall be to goe to wished grave   55
Which is the onlie happie chance I ever wishe to have
That then the passenger may reade in going by
For true and honest constant love, this patient here does
    lye.

---

[1] Orig., *then*. Correction possibly by James.   [2] Rait, *it*.
[3] Rait, *a curs*, an emendation of MS. *ocurs*.

[XV] [1]

My muse hath made a willfull lye I grante,
I sung of sorrows never felt by me;
I have as great occasion for to vante,
My love begunne my blessing for to be.
5 How can I then excuse so lowd a lye?
O yes, I did it even at her desire,
Who made me such successe in love to see,
How soone her flames hade sett my hart on fire.
Since for her sake I presse for to aspire
10 To preache of passions which I never prov'd;
What should yee doe who have for haplesse hire
The lucklesse lott, to love and not be lov'd.
    Your plaints I thinke should pierce the starrie skies
  .And deave the Gods with shrill and cairfull cries.

[XVI]

A COMPLAINT OF HIS MISTRESSIS [2] ABSENCE FROM COURT :—

Whill as a statelie fleeting castle faire
On smoothe and glassie salt does softlie slide
With snowie sheets all flaffing here and thaire
So deck'd and trim'd as she were Neptunes bride
5 And no ways troubled with contrarious tide
And shining Titan from his firie cart
Smiles seing nature triumph'd of by art.

And whill the foolish pilgrims of the seas
Inflam'd with following fortunes fickle baite
10 Esteemes them selfs to be at such an ease
As who bot they into there owen concaite
And everie man sturs up his fellowe maite
As citiezens of Thetis sliprie grounde
And sonnes to Phœbus lightner of this rounde.

Thus whill they thinke there fortune frames at will   15
The Sunne his beames aboundantlie bestowes
Upon the aire to make it cleare and still
The sea so calme as scarcelie ebbs or flowes
No messager of prison'd Æole blowes
Except a gaile with breathing to and fra   20
To stoppe the saile from rashing on the ray.

Then if a cloude the sonne of vapours grosse
Eclipse the Sunne from there astonish'd sight
There cause of joye becumes there cause of losse.
For looke how soone they lacke there former light   25
In place of Phœbus cumes a darckned night
And drumlie cloudes with rumbling thunders rearde
Doe threaten mixing heavens with sea and earde.

O miserable wretches woulde they crie
Who setled trust on so unsetled grounde   30
Who woulde all other elements defie
For that which onelie is unconstant founde
Now were we happie, now into a stounde
Are we ou'rladen with a hell of frayes
Bot warre the rockes, soone cast her in the stayes.   35

O heavenlie lampe Apollo bright and cleare
What crime hath so incenst thy heavenlie ire
For as thy presence made us heavenlie here
Our light, our joye, our comfortable fire
Now loathe we that which most we did desire   40
Since by thy absence heaven in hell is changed
And we as Divells in Plutoes court are ranged.

The like, ô not the like bot like and more
Doe we not one bot all in Court sustaine
Since [1] she who did our Princelie Court decore   45
Is [2] absent, absent doth allace remaine
Whose comelie beautie graced [3] our Princelie traine

[1] Orig., *When.*   [2] Orig., *does.*   [3] Orig., *stain'd.*

Whose modest mirth express'd alluring grace
Whose absence makes us lacke our light allace.

50 The Court as garland lackes the cheefest floure
The Court a chatton toome that lackes her stone
The Court is like a volier at this houre
Wherout of is her sweetest Sirene gone.
Then shall we lacke our cheefest onlie one?
55 No, pull not from us cruell cloude I praye
Our light, our rose, our gemme, our bird awaye.

Bot houpe beginnes to hoise me on her wings
Even houpe that presence absence shall amend.
Bot what my Muse, how pertlie thus thou sings
60 Who rather ought Solsequium like attend
With luckned leaves till wearie night take end.
Haste golden Titan thy so long'd returne
To cleare the skies where now we darckned murne.

[XVII]

A DREAME ON HIS MISTRIS MY LADIE GLAMMES :—

Whill as the silent shaddie night
  Did with her courtens blacke
Ou'rcover Rheas fruictfull face
  And being colde and wacke
5   By sympathie with mortall braines
  Our members make of leade
And stealing all our senses make
  Us lye awhile as deade.
Then whill I was in this estate
10   The God with golden wings,
Who entring at the ports of horne
  So manie monstres brings,
And changing into sundrie shapes
  By strange and subtle slight,
15   Does make us heare without our eares

And see but eyes of light.
This strange and subtle God, I saye
  Of late appear'd to me,
And by the hand my Mistres ledd,
  Loe here she is quoth he,   20
Whose presence breeds as manie joyes
  As absence breeds thee woes [1]
Loe here the harbour of thy hart
  Loe here thy onlie chose [2]
Loe here she is who makes thee trade [3]   25
  The statelie forcked hill,
Whose pleasant grasse beginnes to fade [4]
  So trampled by thee still,
Loe here she is who makes thee drinke
  The christall silver spring   30
Of flying horse and riding foule
  As ancient Poëts sing,
Loe here the subject and the wings
  Of thy high flying verse
That mountes above the flammie vaults   35
  And to the heaven does pearse.
With this me thought she bowed her doune
  And joyned the rubies sine,
(That hides her ivorie rankes and smells
  Of Nectar) unto mine,   40
Sine with her soft and silken hands
  About my necke she layes
A tablet and [5] an Amethyst
  And silent slipps her wayes.
But loe my minde so passion'd was   45
  My hart so sturr'd withall
With joye extreame, as made them soone
  My senses to recall.
And looke how soone from slugglish sleepe
  I perfectlie awooke,   50
Even at the first (ô miracle)

[1] Orig., *noyeis*.   [2] Orig., *choise*.   [3] Orig., *tredd*.
    [4] Orig., *feade*.   [5] Orig., *good*.

Into my hand I tooke
These tokens hunge about my necke
  (As I had dream'd before)
What Deitie (quoth I amaz'd)
  For this shall I adore:
Sume God or Angell suirlie hath
  This present to me brought,
For if on anie naturall dreames
  Hade ravished bene my thought,
Then ather of the humours foure
  The cheefe that did abounde,
By sympathie with brethren foure
  Wherof was form'd this rounde,
And with the seasons of the yeare
  Wolde vexed have my braine.
If bloode domin'd with bloodie jarres
  In spring time, and againe,
If cholere raign'd with ravening fires
  In sommers pearching heate,
If phlegme did with drowning floods
  When Hyades holds there seate,
If melancholie earth and night
  With heavie things and blacke,
When frozen Saturne rules with snowe
  The place wolde suirlie take:
Or els the things I last hade thought
  Hade done or wish'd to be
They hade although imperfectlie
  In dreame appear'd to me.
And so by nature hade I dream'd
  The thing I dream'd indeede,
For I confesse that Idee oft
  My ravish'd minde dois feede,
Bot then how soone I hade awack'd
  And Morpheus flowen awaye,
No token hade he left behinde
  As now this wedd it laye:
Then counting it sume heavenlie gift

And sent me from above,   90
I cust me narrowlie to guesse
   What coulde the meaning prove,
And so beganne both up and doune
   To tosse, to viewe, to spie —
This tablet and the Amethyst   95
   There secrets for to trie.
Thou Lycian Lord that Deitie
   Whome Delphos did adore,
Whose shining coache doe saphirs blewe
   And rubies red decore,   100
The sacred Sisters Monarch greate,
   The spirit that did inspire
With oracles the Sybills sage
   Inflam'd with heavenlie fire,
O thou that mysteries can reveale   105
   And future things foreseis
Assist my seeking out of this
   And open cleare mine eyes.
The Amethyst in forme of hart
   Doeth sign'fie the hart   110
And constant love unchangeable
   That is upon my part,
And as the colours of this stone
   Are purple mix'd with graye,
So flames of love my earthlie parts   115
   Consumes me day by daye.
The secret vertues that are hidd
   Into this pretious stone
Indues me with meete qualities
   For serving such a one,   120
For as this stone by secret force
   Can soveraignlie remeade
These daizeled braines whome Bacchus strength
   Ou'rcomes as they were deade,
And can preserve us from the harme   125
   Of the envenomed sting
Of poysoned cuppes, that to our tombe

Untymelie does us bring,
So shall my hart be still preserved
130   By vertue from above,
From staggering like a drunken man
    Or wavering into love:
Bot by this soveraigne antidote
    Of her whom still I serve
135 In spite of all the poysoned lookes
    Of Dames I shall not swerve.
And speciallie with courage bolde
    This stone can furnish me
That with my conquering hand I may
140   Enforce my foes to flie,
For suire he can not worthie be
    To be accompted deare
By anie Dame that in his brest
    A womans hart dois beare.
145 And therfor for my part I vowe
    If as the rumours be
Of jarrs and broyles, I happen in
    Effect the same to see,
I shall not from the enemies sight
150   To anie part remove,
Unkithing once in honour of
    My Mistres and my love:
Bot onlie mot I conquered be
    And onelie will I yeelde
155 To Cupids shott, whose firie darts
    Resist coulde never sheelde.
And lastlie as this stone hath force
    A hunter for to aide,
In end to catche his pray, the fruict
160   Of all his travell made,
So as I am an prentise past
    Into that Princelie game,
Whose hounds and horns through rockes and woodes
    Makes Echo answer them,
165 I trust by vertue of this stone

To winne and holde the pray
That prayes on me, and is of all
  My passion'd thoughts the stay.
Bot loe I long to turne me to
  The tablet made of golde,   170
And all without and in the same
  At length for to beholde.
Of purest golde the tablet made
  Which by the fire is fin'd,
Her chastnes pure does represent   175
  In bodie both and mind,
The crawling scores of ameling blacke
  That on the golde are wrought,
The divers passions represents
  That walters in her thought.   180
One of the leaves on utter side
  A nacked man does beare,
Whome Phœbus rosts with hote reflexe
  And stinging flees doe teare.
Yett sitting in the forrest greene,   185
  As senceles of his harme,
By harmonie of violl sweete
  He never irkes to charme
The ravish'd foules and beasts about,
  Esteeming so there joye,   190
As makes him quite for to forgett
  His grievous sore anoye.
This man not onelie represents
  Her Siren voyce divine,
Wherewith she makes the dullest eares   195
  And hardest harts encline,
Bot as his dittie sayes, To please
  The rest he suffers paine,
So she her Princesse serves of love
  Without respect of gaine.   200
The other on the utter side
  The Sunne hath shining bright
Into the midst, with stars about

2

Bot darckned by his light
205 And as that dittie sayes, As Sunne
Amongst the stars does shine,
So she her sexe surpasseth far
In vertues most divine:
That Sunne of whome I sung before
210 Whose absence made me flie
Above the skies, ô Sunne to seeke
Her shaddowe into the.
Bot if into these former verse
I soar'd with Eagle wings,
215 Then Mistres thanke your selfe for them
That by your vertue sings.
Bot greatest comfort is to me
To spie the inward part,
Wheras ane hand does holde me thinke
220 My onelie Mistres hart,
Whill Cupide with his bended bowe
And golden arrowe aime,
To shoote his subtle firie shaft
For pearcing of the same:
225 Bot that her hand does holde her hart
I take it for to be,
That willinglie she letts her hart
Be shotte into for me.
The inward of the other leafe
230 It emptie does remaine,
Which if my guesse deceave me not,
Is ordain'd to containe,
The art of sume Apelles fine,
The portraict of her face,
235 To give unto the workemanship
Of all the rest a grace:
For as the rest does represent
Her qualities most rare,
So shoulde her selfe, though vivelie, no,
240 Yett best it can be there.
And suire the Gods above they have

Decreed as seemes to me,
That as the tablet and the stone,
    Both knitt together be
Even by a string, the tablet like   245
    To her, to me the stone,
So shall our love whill Atrope cutt
    The threed, be knitt in one.
Thus have I redd my dreme ye see
    With wise Apollos aide,   250
And if this be the verrie trueth
    That I herin have saide,
Then am I gladd of such a guesse,
    Bot if I be deceav'd,
And in the opening of a dreame   255
    Have ather dream'd or reav'd
Yett wellcume be a gladd deceate,
    For as into my sleepe,
My dreame deceaved [1] me, so my guesse,
    In gladnes doth me keepe.   260
Now may ye see ô Titan mine,
    No distance far of place,
Nor other thoughts can out of me
    The thought of you deface,
In absence are ye present still   265
    And ever so in sight,
No wonder is, what Monarch may
    Resist a womans might.

[XVIII]

A SATIRE AGAINST WOEMEN [2]

As falcons are by nature faire of flight
Of kinde as sparhalks far excells in speede
As marlions [3] have in springing greatest might

---

[1] Orig., *ravish'd*. Altered by James.
[2] Printed in Rait, with the supplied title, *On Women*.
[3] Rait, *martrones;* glossed, *martens*.

As gosehalks are of nature given to greede
5 As mavises of kinde are given to sing
And lavrocks after candlemasse to spring.

As piots steales what ever they can beare
Of kinde as corbies followes carions vilde
As jeas will conterfitt what sounde they heare
10 As gledds of nature kills not oft the wylde
As crowes and kaes will clatter when they playe
As hens of nature keckells when they laye.

As kinde makes hounds to followe hairs by sent
As cursours nickers riding in the night
15 As lions for to seeke there praye are bent
As beares by kinde, of leggs are wonderous wight
As tigres flies the waters and the wites
As nature gives the Ounces cruell sprites.

As goates delights to climbe through craige and cleughe
20 As deere of nature hants the forrest faire
As conns by kinde will skippe from branche to beughe
As foxes can by craft escaipe the snaire
As brockes in winter likes to sleepe and rest
As swine by nature loves the midding best.

25   As schooles of herring flees the whaill for feare
As greate olde pyckes will eate the young and small
As remora will stoppe a shippe to steare
As kinde makes sea horse to be cruell all
As kinde makes crevises to swimme abacke
30 As troutes of nature fishers baits will take.

As marmaides hates all men by natures will
As delphins loves all bairns in wonderous sorte
As by the contrare crocodills them kill
As mareswines loves of nature for to sporte

Of kinde as salmon in freshe water [1] spawnes   35
As selchs have milke and young ons lacking rawnes.[2]

In short as foules by kinde in aire doe flee
And as the beasts by nature goes [3] on grounde
And as the fishes swimmes in frothie see
And as all living things are ever bounde   40
To followe nature ruling them allwaye
Whose will obeye thay must butt lett or staye.

Even so all wemen are of nature vaine
And can not keepe no secrett unrevealed
And where as once they doe concaive disdaine   45
They are unable to be reconcealed
Fullfild with talke and clatters but respect
And often tymes of small or none effect.

Ambitious all without regarde or shame
Butt anie measure given to greede of geare   50
Desyring ever for to winne a name
With flattering all that will them not forbeare
Sume craft they have, yett foolish are indeede
With lying whiles esteeming best to speede.

Exposition [4]

Expone me right ye Dames of worthie fame   55
Since for your honours I employed my caire
For wemen bad hereby are lesse to blame
For that they followe nature everie whaire
And ye most worthie prayse, whose reason dants
That nature, which into your sexe, so hants.   60

---

[1] Rait, *riueris.*
[2] Rait, *& young onis laik in graunis;* glossed, "as young seals play in branches of rivers."
[3] Rait, *go.*
[4] Rait, *Excuise.*

[XIX]

SONG I [1]

What mortall man may live but hart
As I doe now suche is my cace
For now the whole is from the part
Devided eache in divers place
5   The seas are now the barr
    Which makes us distant farr
    That we may soone winne narr
        God graunte us grace.

Full manie causes suire I have
10   Which does augment my woe and caire
Bot one more speciall nor the leave
When I doe thinke what joye was thaire
    What gladnes and what greeting
    At our long wished meeting
15   I can not well unwiting [2]
        My cheekis declare.

And sine how we so soone were shedd
And loste our long desired joye
O what mischance, I never redd
20   That lovers hade suche cause of noye
    For other lovers uses
    The one to make excuses
    Of absence, thus abuses
        Them Venus boye.

25   Bot we endure far greater skaith
For onelie one of them hath paine
Bot we alike are wounded baith
And cairfull till we meete againe

---

[1] Title in the handwriting of Charles. Printed in Rait, with the last two stanzas first, and the supplied title, *Bot be the Contraire I Reiose.*
[2] Rait, *I can not ueill on ueitting;* glossed, "without wetting."

O absence cruell foe
Why workes thou us such woe   30
And gars true lovers so
    Far shedd remaine.

Thou absence gives me cause to feare
Lest she be harm'd by sume mischance
       makes   long
Thou absence gars me greine [1] to heare   35
Some worde from her, thou gars me panse
    What waye for to eschewe
    These sorrowes which renewe
    And whiles I change my hewe
        Whiles falls in transe.   40

Bot by the contrare I rejoyes
When I persave we marrowes be
In trouble, sorrowe and in noyes
That is a thing which comforts me
    The proverbe makes relation   45
    That likes in tribulation
    Is wretches consolation
        So now are we.

Rejoyce therfor my halfe in all [2]
Since honest causes be the staye,   50
Of presence, houpe that meete we shall
With greater gladnes on a daye.
    I praye the Lord abone
    To send it till us soone
    Farewell till that be done   55
        And after aye.

---

[1] *Eligat lector* is written in the margin in the hand of James. Rait, *garris me greine.*

[2] Rait has *lenuoy* above this stanza.

[XX]

SONG 2 [1]

When as the skillfull archer false
Inflam'd and pearc'd by craftie arte
Leanders hart and Heros als
By his so firie golden darte
5   Fra Cupide blinde assailde
        With bowe and shaft
        His will they never failde
        Such was his craft.

And ever from that tyme agoe
10   There love to others never past
Whill fortune was there mortall foe
And made them perishe both at last
        The raging seas they war
        Twixt them a barr
15   There cheefest toyle and caire
        To swimme so farr.

Bot liker is my fortune raire
Since seas divydes us not at all
To Piramus and Thisbe faire
20   Devyded onlie by a wall
        Which in it hade a bore
        Wherethrough they spake
        Which of a chance before
        Dame fortune brake.

25   The verrie like did us befall
As them of whome I shewe before
We distant are by such a wall
And often spacke by such a bore
        Whill envie called a naile
30   There through so strate
        As made our moyen faile
        To speake of late.

1 Title in the handwriting of Charles.

MISCELLANEA

[XXI] [1]

Ad hoc creaturæ destinatæ sunt, ut in eis glorificetur Creator.

The azured vault, the cristall circles bright [2]
The gleaming firie torches poudered thair
The changing rounde, the shining beamie light
The sadd and bearded fires, the monsters faire
The prodiges appearing in the aire   5
The rearding thunders and the blustering windes
The foules in hewe, in shape and nature rare
The prettie notts that wing'd musiciens findes
In earthe the savourie flowres, the metall'd mindes
The wholesome herbes, the hautie pleasant trees   10
The silver streames, the beasts of sundrie kindes
The bounded roares, and fishes of the seas
    All these for teaching man the Lord did frame
    To honoure him [3] whose glorie shines in them.

[XXII]

A SONNET ON M[R] PA. ADAMSONS PARAPHRASE OF JOB : [4] —

In wandring wealth through burbling [5] brookes and bewes
Of tripping troupes and flocks on fertill grounde
In cattell great of sundrie shapes and hewes
With hovves [6] all whole, or in a parted rounde

---

[1] Crossed out in the MS., with the note: "This sonnet is printed at the end of Lepanto." [*Exercises at vacant houres.*]

[2] Orig., *christal skies and bright.*

[3] Exercises, *To do his will.* The change is made by James.

[4] Crossed out at this point in the MS., but inserted on fol. 45 *b.* It was published in *Adamsoni Poemata Sacra*, London, 1619, and is printed in Irving's *Lives of the Scotish Poets*, Vol. II, p. 222, with the fifth line omitted.

[5] Fol. 45 *b, bubbling.*

[6] Fol. 45 *b, hooffes.*

5   In fields fullfild [1] with cornes by sheavers bounde
In heapes of golde, and ritches in all wayes
As Job excelled all others might be founde
Of Monarchs greate or Princes in his dayes
So this translatour merites no less praise
10 For gifts of sprite, then he for gifts of geare
And God in grace hath given such counterpaise
As his translation to the worke is peere
    God did his gifts in him [2] so wiselie mell
    Whose heavenlie wealth Jobs earthlie wealth doth tell.

[XXIII]

A SONNET ON TICHO BRAHE : —

That onlie essence who made all of noght
Our great and mightie Lord the life of all
When he in ordour everie thing hade broght
At the creating of this earthlie ball
5   Then made he man at last. Thy raigne it shall
Extend (quod Jehova) in everie cace
Over all these breathing beasts that flatlie fall
For humble hommage here before thy face
He also pitch'd eache Planet in his place
10 And made them rulers of the ruling Lord
As heavenlie impes to governe bodies basse
Be subtle and celestiall sweete accord
    Then greate is Ticho who by this his booke
    Commandement doth ouer these commanders brooke.

[XXIV]

ANOTHER ON THE SAME : —

The glorious globe of heavenlie matter made
Containing ten celestiall circles faire
Where shining starres in glistring graithe arraide
Most pleasantlie are poudered here and thair

---

[1] Fol. 45 b, *fulle filld.*
[2] Fol. 45 b, Irving, *God did in him his gifts.*

Where everie planet hath his owen repaire 5
And christall house, a whirling wheill in rounde
Whose calme aspects or froward does declaire
Gods minde to blisse great kingdomes or confounde
Then if you list to see on earthlie grounde
There ordour, course, and influence appeare 10
Looke Tichoes tooles, there finelie shall be founde
Eache planet dansing in his propre spheare
There fires divine into his house remaine
Whome sommerlie his booke doth here containe.

[XXV]

ANOTHER ON THE SAME : —

What foolish Phaëton did presume in pride
Yea more what great Apollo takes in hand
Who does the course of glistring Phœbus guide
Thou does performe that rules eache firie brand
Then greater art thou then Apollo cleare 5
As thy Uranias eldest fostre deare.

[XXVI]

A SONNET ON DU BARTAS [1]

Since ye [2] immortall sisters nine have [3] left
All other countries lying far or neere
To follow him who from you all them reft [4]
And now hath caused your residence be here
Who thogh a stranger, yett he lov'd so deere 5
This realme and me, so as he spoil'd his awin
(And all the brookes, the bankes and fontains cleere
That be in it) of you, as he hath shawin

---

[1] Printed in *The Historie of Judith in forme of a Poeme: penned in French by the noble poet G. Sallust, Lord of Bartas: Englished by Tho. Hudson*, Edin., 1584. Printed in the 1608 and later editions of Sylvester.
[2] Orig., *the.*
[3] Orig., *hath.*
[4] Orig., Hudson, *from them all you reft*

In this youre [1] worke, then let your breaths be blawin
10 In recompense of this his willing minde
On me, that then may with my penn be drawin
His praise: who [2] thogh him selfe be not inclin'd
    Nor preasseth but to touche the laurell tree
    Yett well he merites crown'd therwith to be.

[XXVII]

What heaven doth furnish thee such learned skill
What heavenly fire inspires thy furious sprite
What foule bereaves thou for to painte at will
Thy travells greate, what booke gives floures most sweete
5 Deck'd, holie, cleane, alone but matches meete
Wise, loftie, learned, with good will florish'd faire
Of penn, of brightnes, smell and skill compleete
They wonder at thee in heaven, fire, earthe, and aire
Great God who heares from heaven his cantiques raire
10 And knowes thy harper, furie, pen, and floure
Preserve him in his midrinke with thy caire
But doubt his skill will change in heaven sume houre
    His soule in starre, his furie in fires most strange
    His pen in Phœnix, corps in floure shall change.

[XXVIII] [3]

O divin du Bartas, disciple d'Uranie
L'Honneur de nostre temps, poëte du grand Dieu
Tes saincts vers doux-coulants pleins de douce manie
Distillés des hauts cieux volent de lieu en lieu
5 Comme esclairs foudroyants du grand esprit tonnant
Postillonent tonnants du levant au ponant.

[XXIX]

A SONNET ON MR W. FULLERS TRANSLATION OF PETRARCHS
TRIUMPHE OF LOVE:[1] —

We find by proofe that into everie age
In Phœbus art sume glistring starre[2] did shine
Who worthie schollers to the Muses sage
Fulfil'd there countries with there workes divine
So Homere was a sounding trumpett fine   5
Amongst the Greeks into his learned dayes
So Virgill was amongst the Romanes sine
A spirit sublimed, a piller of there praise
So loftie Petrarch his renoume did blaze
In toungue Italique in a sugred stile   10
And to the circled skies his name did raise
For he by poëms that he did compile
  In triumphe ledde[3] love, chastness, deathe, and fame
  Bot thou triumphes ouer Petrarchs propre name.

[XXX]

AN EPITAPHE ON S^R PHILIP SIDNEY:[4] —

Thou mightie Mars the God[5] of souldiours brave
And thou Minerve that does in witt excell
And thou Apollo that does knowledge have
Of everie art that from Parnassus fell
With all the[6] Sisters that theron doe dwell   5
Lament for him who dewlie serv'd you all
Whome in, you wiselie all your arts did mell
Bewaile I say his unexpected fall

---

[1] Printed in Leyden's *Scotish Descriptive Poems*. Printed from Leyden
in Gillies' reprint of *The Essayes of a Prentise*, Preface, p. vii.
  [2] Leyden, *stars.*
  [3] Orig., Leyden, *Ledde in triumphe.* Correction by Carey.
  [4] Printed in *Academiæ Cantabrigensis Lachrymæ Tumulo . . . Sidneii.*
. . . London, 1587.
  [5] Acad., *Lord.*
  [6] Acad., *your.*

I neede not in remembrance for to call
10 His youth, his race,[1] the houpe hade of him aye
Since that in him doeth cruell deathe appall
Both manhoode, witt, and learning everie waye
Now in the bed of honour doeth he rest [2]
And evermore of him shall live the best.

[XXXI]

AN EPITAPHE ON JOHN SHAW : —

A vertuous life procures a happie deathe
And raires to loftie skies there noble name
Then blest is he who looseth thus his breathe
Though to his friends it be a griefe the same.
5 This may be saide of thy immortal fame
Who here reposes closed in honours laire
For as of trewe and noble race thou came
So honestie and trueth was all thy caire
Thy kinn was honoured by thy vertues raire
10 Thy place of creditt did thy friends defend.
Then noble mindes aspire and doe not spaire
With such a life to conquise such an end
Bot here my inward greefe does make me staye
I minde with deeds, and not with wordes to paye.

[XXXII]

VOTUM

Thy kindenes kithed in loosing life for me
My kindnesse on thy friends I utter shall
My perrill kindled courage into the
Mine shall revenge thy saikles famous fall
5 Thy constant service ever shall remaine
As freshe with me as if thou lived againe.

[1] Acad., *His race, his youth.*
[2] Acad., *But yet he doth in bed of honor rest.*

[XXXIII]

A SONNET TO CHANCELLER MAITLANE : —

Vigiliæ nostræ.

If he who valliant even within the space
That Titan six times twise his course does end
Did conquise olde Dame Rheas fruictfull face
And did his raigne from pole to pole extend
Hade thought him happier if that greeke hade penn'd   5
His worthie praise who traced the Trojane sacke
Then all his actes that forth his fame did send
Or his triumphant trophees might him make.
Then what am I that on Pegasian backe
Does flee amongs the Nymphes immortall faire   10
For thou ô Maitland does occasion take
Even by my verse to spreade my name allwhere
    For what in barbarous leide I blocke and frames
    Thou learnedlie in Minerv's tongue proclames.

Olet lucernam certé, nam cum lucerna excogitatum fuit.

[XXXIV]

AN EPITAPHE ON MONTGOMRIE : —

What drousie sleepe doth syle [1] your eyes allace
Ye sacred brethren of Castalian band
And shall the prince of Poëts in our land
Goe thus to grave unmurned in anie cace
No ; whett your pens ye imps of heavenlie grace   5
And toone me up your sweete resounding strings
And mounte him so on your immortall wings
That ever he may live in everie place
Remember on Montgomries flowand grace
His suggred stile his weightie words divine   10

[1] Orig., *fill.*

And how he made the sacred Sisters nine
There montaine quitte to followe on his trace
   Though to his buriall was refused the bell
   The bell of fame, shall aye his praises knell.

[XXXV]

A SONNET ON THE MONETH OF MAY : —

Haill mirthfull May the moneth full of joye
Haill mother milde of hartsume herbes and floures
Haill fostrer faire of everie sporte and toye
And of Auroras dewis and summer shoures
5 Haill friend to Phœbus and his glancing houres
Haill sister scheine to Nature breeding all
Who by the raine that cloudie skies out pouris
And Titans heate, reformes the faided fall
In woefull winter by the frostie gall
10 Of sadd Saturnus tirrar of the trees
And now by Natures might and thine they shall
Be florish'd faire with colours that agrees
   Then lett us all be gladd to honour the
   As in olde tymes was ever wonte to be.

[XXXVI] [1]

AN ÆNIGME OF SLEEPE : —

Life is my selfe, I keepe the life of all
Without my helpe all living things they die
Small, greate, poore, ritche, obeye unto my call
Feirce lions, foules, and whaills into the sie
5 With meete and drinke the hungrie I supplie
Deade drunken als I quicken newe againe
Dearer to Kings, nor crownes and sceptours hie
Unto the riche, nor all there wealth and gaine
I am not nyse, the poore I'le not disdaine
10 Poore wretches more then Kings may me command

[1] Crossed out in the MS.

Where I cumme in all senses man refraine
Softer nor silke, and sadder nor the sand
 I hurt, I helpe, I slaye, and cuire the same
 SLEEPE, and advise, and panse well what I am.

[XXXVII]

A SONNET WHEN THE KING WAS SURPRISED BY THE EARLE BOTHWELL[1]

A faschious fight does force my freest minde
Betwixt two valliant champions I persave
The one trewe courage rightlie is defin'd
The other wisedome temperat and grave
Thy selfe undanted showe quoth courage brave   5
Bot wisedome wishes for a while to staye
Quoth courage rather die then live a slave
Quoth wisedome true, if so should be for aye
Bot wracke the not upon thy selfe I praye
Since keeping up thy selfe bot for a space   10
On others sine thy courage kithe thou may
Quoth courage, lingring is a great disgrace
 Of all these straits the best is out of doubte
 That courage wise, and wisedome shoulde [2] be stoute.

[XXXVIII]

ANOTHER ON THE SAME : —

Shall treason then of trueth have the rewarde
And shall rebellion thus exalted be
Shall cloked vice with falsehoods fained farde
In creditt creepe and glister in our eye
Shall coloured knaves so malapertlie lie   5
And shamelesse sowe there poysoned smitting seede
And shall perjured infamous foxes slie
With there triumphes make honest harts to bleede

[1] The title is an alteration in the hand of Carey. The original is too obliterated to read.
[2] Orig., *shall.*

3

How long shall Furies on our fortunes feede
10 How long shall vice her raigne possesse in rest
How long shall Harpies our displeasure breede
And monstrous foules sitt sicker in our nest
   In tyme appointed God will suirlie have
   Eache one his due rewarde for to resave.

[XXXIX] [1]

All kinde of wronge allace it now aboundes
And honestie is fleemed out of this land
Now trumprie over trueth his triumphe soundes
Who now can knowe the hart by tongue or hand
5 Cummes ever justice at the barre to stande
Where can she be in these our later dayes
Alike in water for to wagg a wande
As speare for her if truelie sundrie sayes
For manie now abroade doe daylie blaize
10 That justice hath her hart infected sore
How can she then be cleane in anie wayes
Bot must become corrupted more and more
   Sume lockman now hath locked up apart
   Poore justice martyr'd with a meschant hart.

[XL]

A SONNET PAINTING OUT THE PERFECT POËT [2]

A ripe ingine, a quicke and walkened witt
With summaire raisons suddainlie applied
For everie purpose using raisons fitt
With skillfulnes where learning may be spied
5 With pitthie wordes for to expresse you by it
His full intention in his propre leide
The propertie wherof well hes he tryit
With memorie to keepe what he doth reide

---

[1] Crossed out in the MS.
[2] Crossed out in the MS., with the note: "This sonnet is alreadie printed
and prefixed to the treatise of Scottish poesie." [*Essayes of a Prentise.*]

With skillfulnes and figures which proceede
From rhetorick, with everlasting fame   10
With others wondering preassing with all speede
For to attaine to merite such a name
    All these into the perfect Poëte be
    Gods grante I may attaine the laurell tree.

[XLI] [1]

A SONNET TO THE READER PREFIXED TO THE TREATISE OF
THE ART OF POESIE [2]

Since for your sake I wrytte upon your art
Apollo, Pan, and ye ô Muses nine
And thou ô Mercure for to helpe thy part
I the [3] emplore since thou by thy ingine
Nixt after Pan hade founde the whissell, sine   5
Thou did perfect that, which he bot espied
And after that made Argos for to tine
Who keeped Io, all his windowes by it
Concurre ye Gods I [4] can not be denied
Since of your art of poësie I writte   10
That birds will learne [5] by teaching it is tried
Sic docens discam, if ye helpe to dicte
    Then reader see of nature thou have part
    Sine lackes thou noght, bot here to reade the art.

[XLII] [6]

O mightie [7] Gods since I with pen and poëts art
So willinglie hath serv'd you thogh my skill be small
I praye you [8] everie one of you to helpe his part
In granting this my suite which after followe shall.

---

[1] Crossed out in MS., with the note, "This sonnet is prefixed to the treatise of Scottish poesie and is alreadie printed."

[2] Orig., *treatise of scottish poësie.* Correction by James.

[3] Essayes, *do.*   [4] Essayes, *it.*

[5] Orig., *Olde birdes do learne.* Correction by James.

[6] MS. note: "These two following sonnetts with the preface, are printed." All three are crossed out.   [7] Essayes, *Immortall.*   [8] Essayes, *then.*

[XLIII]

First Jove as greatest God above the rest
Grante thou to me a part of my desire
That when of the in verse [1] I writte my best
This onlie thing of the I doe require [2]
5   That thou my vaine poëtick so enspire
As they may surelie thinke all that it reede
When I describe thy might and thundring fire
That they doe see thy selfe in verrie deede
From heavens thy greatest thunders for to leade
10   And sine upon the Giants heads to fall
Or cumming to thy Semele with speede
In thunders least at her request and call
    Or throwing Phaëton doune from heaven to earde
    With threatning thunders make a monstrous rearde.

[XLIV]

Apollo nixt assist me to [3] a part
Since thou are second unto Jove [4] in might
That when I like describe thy heavenlie cart [5]
The readers may esteeme it in there sight
5   And grante me als the worlds ô onlie light
Whome on the yeare, with seasons double twise
Do waite: that so I may describe it right [6]
That so I may describe the verrie guise
By thy good [7] helpe of yeares wherein we live

---

[1] Essayes, *that when in verse of thee.*
[2] Essayes, *This onely thing I earnestly requyre.*
[3] Essayes, *in.*
[4] Essayes, *unto Jove thou secound art.*
[5] Essayes. *I do descryve thy shyning Carte.*
[6] In altering the sonnet as printed in the Essayes, a line was lost altogether.
Cf. Essayes, ll. 6-9 : —
        That when I lyke for subject to devyse
        To wryte, how as before thy countenaunce bright
        The yeares do stand, with seasons double twyse,
        That so I may descryve the verrie guyse, etc.
[7] Essayes, *Thus by thy.*

As readers sine may saye here suirlie lyis 10
Of seasons foure the glasse and picture vive
And grante [1] that so I may my verses warpe
As thou may playe them sine upon thy harpe.

[XLV] [2]

O mightie sonne of Semele the faire
O Bacchus borne by Jove the God of might
O twise borne boye, who ever does, and dare
Subdue all mortall with thy liquour wight
Who with thy power blinded hath [3] the sight 5
To sume, to others thou the eares have deaffed
From sume thou takes the taste, sume smelling right
Doeth lacke, sume touching, sume all five bereaved
Are of thee,[4] the greate Alexandre craved
Thy mercie oft, our maistre poëte now 10
Is warde by the ; we smaller then sall leave it
To strive with the.   Then on his tombe I vowe
Shall be, Here lyis whome Bacchus by his wyne
Hath trapped first, and made him render sine.

[XLVI]

A SONNETT ON S[R] WILLIAM ALEXANDER'S HARSHE
VERSES AFTER THE INGLICHE FASONE [5]

Hould [6] hould your hand, hould, mercy, mercy, spare
Those sacred nine that nurst you many a yeare

---

[1] Essayes, *Grant als.*

[2] Crossed out in the MS.   Printed in Rait, with the supplied title, *Sonnet to Bacchus.*   Rait notes its reference to Montgomerie, though not the fact that it indicates his death.

[3] Rait, *blindithes.*   [4] Rait omits *thee.*

[5] Title and poem in the hand of Carey.   Printed in *The Earl of Stirling's Register of Royal Letters relative to the affairs of Scotland and Nova Scotia from 1615 to 1635,* ed. Rev. Charles Rogers, Edin., 1885, Introd., p. xi, from a MS. in the collection of Sir David Balfour in the Advocates Lib. Rogers has the following title : *The Complainte of the Muses to Alexander upon him selfe, for his ingratitude towards them, by hurting them with his hard hammered wordes, fitter to be used upon his mineralles.*   [6] Rog., O.

Full oft alas with comfort and with care
Wee bath'd you in Castalias fountaine [1] cleare
5   Then on our winges aloft wee did you beare
And set you on our stately forked hill
Where [2] you our heavnly harmonyes did heare
The rockes resoundinge with there Echoes still
Although your neighbours have conspir'd to spill [3]
10   That art which [4] did the Laurel crowne obtaine
And [5] borowing from the raven there ragged quill
Bewray there harsh, hard [6] trotting tumbling wayne
   Such hamringe hard the [7] metalls hard require
   Our songs are fil'd with smoothly flowing [8] fire.

[XLVII]

A SONET AGAINST THE COULD THAT WAS IN JANUARY 1616 [9]

How cruely these catiffs doe conspire
What loathsome love breeds such a baleful band,
Betwixt the cancred Kinge of Creta land
That melancholy ould and angry syre
5   And him who wont to quench debaite and ire
Amongst the Romains when his ports were clos'd
But now his double face is still dispos'd
With Saturns helpe to freeze us at the fire
The earth or'e-covered with a sheete of snow
10   Refuses foode to foule to bird and beast
The chillinge cold letts every thing to grow
And surfets cattil with a starving feast

---

[1] Rog., *founteyns.*
[2] Rog., *When.*
[3] Rog., *kill.*
[4] Rog., *that.*
[5] Rog., *Who.*
[6] Rog., *hard, harsh.*
[7] Rog., *youre.*
[8] Rog., *smooth o'erflowing.* This and *youre* preceding are MS. corrections in the hand of James (Roger's note).
[9] Title and poem in the hand of Carey. Printed in *The Works of William Drummond of Hawthornden*, Edin., 1711, p. 149. Printed from Drummond in *Earl of Stirling's Register of Royal Letters*, Introd., p. xii.

Curst bee that Love and may't [1] continue short
That kills all creaturs and doth spoile our sport.

[XLVIII] [2]

Not orientall Indus cristall streames;
Nor frutfull Nilus, that no bankes can thole;
Nor golden Tagus; wher bright Titans beames,
Ar headlongst hurled, to vew the Antartike Pole;
   Nor Ladon (wch sweet Sidney dothe extole)   5
While it, th' Arcadian Beauties did embrace:
All these cannot, thee, nameless thee, controle;
But, with good right, must rander & give place:
   For, whilst sweete she, voutsafest to show her face,
And, with her presence, honnors thee ilke daye;   10
Thou slyding, seemest, to have a slower pace,
Against thy will, as if thou went away;
   And, loathe to leave, the sight of suche a one
   Thou still imparts, thy plaints, to every stone.

[XLIX] [2]

Faire famous Isle, where Agathocles rang;
Where sometymes, statly Siracusa stood;
Whos fertill feelds, were bathed in bangsters blood
When Rome, & ryvall Carthage, strave so lang:
   Great Ladie Mistriss, all the Isles amang,   5
Which standes in Neptunes, circle mouving, flood;
No, nather for thy frutefull ground nor good;
I chuse the, for the subject of my sang;
   Nor, for the ould report, of scarce trew fame;
Nor heeretofore, for farelies in the found;   10
But, for the sweet resemblance of that Name,
To whom thou seemest, so sibb, at least, in sound;
   If then, for seeming so, thy prays bee such;
   Sweet she her selfe, dothe merit more then much.

---

[1] Drummond, *mought*.   [2] Handwriting of Charles.

[L]

UPON OCCASION OF SOME GREAT DISORDERS IN SCOTLAND [1]

O cruell constellation that conspird
Before my birth my bale sa sharpe & saire
O miserable Mother that desir'd
The Midwife wise na paines on me to spaire
5   In vaine wase milke my meate a yeare & maire
In vaine therafter wase I speand alace
In vaine ye wise Pierides tooke a caire
To bring me bravely up in everie cace
In vaine ye made me syne to take a place
10   Upon that forked hill in honnour hie
In vaine descended I of Royal race
W^{ch} by succession made a King of me
All were but shawes Marcellus sure am I
Or Job whaise patience Sathan thinkes to try.

[LI]

An admonition to the Master poët to be warr of great
bragging hereafter, lest he not onlie slander him selfe;
bot also the whole professours of the art : [2] —

Give patient eare to sumething I man saye
Beloved Sanders maistre of our art
The mouse did helpe the lion on a daye
So I protest ye take it in good part
5   My admonition cumming from a hart
That wishes well to you and all your craft
Who woulde be sorie for to see you smart
Thogh other poëts trowes ye be gone daft.

A friend is aye best knowen in tyme of neede
10   Which is the cause that gars me take such caire

[1] Title in Carey's handwriting, poem in Charles's. Between this and
the Admonition, on fol. 45 *b*, occurs a second insertion, in Charles's hand,
of the *Sonnet on M^r Pa. Adamsons Paraphrase of Job.* Cf. ante, XXII.

[2] The entire poem crossed out in the MS. Printed in Rait, with the title,
Ane Admonition to the Maister Poete to leave of greit crakking.

Now for your state since there is cause indeede
For all the poëts leaves you standing baire
Olde crucked Robert makes of you the haire
And elfegett Polward helpes the smitthie smuike
He comptes you done, and houpes but anie mair 15
His tyme about, to winne the chimnay nuike

Bot as the guid chirurgian oft does use
I meane to rype the wounde before he heal'd
Appardone me I [1] thinke it no excuse
Suppose I tell the cause why they have rail'd 20
And sine considder whither ye have fail'd
Or what hath caus'd them this waye to backbite you
Into that craft they never yett prevail'd
Albeit of late they houpe for to outflite you.

For ye was cracking crouslie of your broune, 25
If Robert lie not, all the other night
That there was anie like him in this toune
Upon the grounde ye wolde not lett it light
He was so firie speedie yaulde and wight
For to be shorte he was an A per se 30
Bot yett beleeve [2] ye saw an other sight
Or all was done (or Robins rithme [3] does lie.

Thus cracked ye and bragged but replie
Or answer made by anie present then
As Dares did, when as he did ou'rhye 35
Eneas court nor could not finde a man
That match him durst; the stirke for him that wann
Which ordain'd was, he craved at Ænes hand
And saide since there is none that doe or can
Be matche to me what longer shall I stand. 40

Delaye no more, bot give me the rewarde
Preordinate for them that victor war

---

[1] Rait, &.   [2] Rait, *beliue.*   [3] Rait, *ryme.*

Thus Dares ended bot Æneas stairde
The campe about, since there is none that darr
45 Æneas saide, bot all seemes verrie skarr
T'essaye [1] yone man gar bring the bullock soone
Thus as he bade they broght the bullocke narr
Which hade his hornes ou'rgilded all [2] abone.

Amongs the armie which were witnes thair
50 And not but wonder harde yone Dares boaste
Entellus raise a man of stature mair
Nor Dares was, and saide cheefe of our hoaste
I now repent my former youthe is loste
Bot since I see he shames your armie so
55 Have at him then, it shall be on his coste
As I beleeve, if Jove be not my foe.

The circumstances of this bargane keene
I will remitt to Virgils ornate stile
Bot well I watt Entellus soone was seene
60 By all to winne: So cracked ye a while
That none might neere you scarcelie by a mile,
Till your Entellus harde you at the last
The daye was sett, bot ye begoode [3] to smile
For scorne, and thought to winne by running fast.

65 The wavering worde did spredde abroade belive
Of all your crackes and bargane that was made
Each one with other bussilie did strive
Who should be soonest at that solemne rade
That they might judge which of the horse shoulde leade
70 Ye saide there woulde no question be of that
Besides ye saide ye caired not all there feade
Brecke as [4] they woulde, the race it should no latt.

That night ye ceis'd and went to bed, bot grien'd
Yett fast for day, and thocht the nicht to lang

----

[1] Rait, *to sey.*　　　　[3] Rait, *begouth.*
[2] Rait, *as.*　　　　　　[4] Rait, *brekis.*

At last Diana doune her heade reclin'd   75
Into the sea, then Lucifer up sprang
Auroras poste whome she did send amang
The gettie cloudes for to foretell ane houre
Before she staye her teares which Ovide sang
Was for her love which turned into a floure.   80

Fra Lucifer hade thus his message done
The rubie virgin came for to forspeeke
Apollos cumming in his glistring throne
Who suddainlie therafter cleare did keeke
Out through his cart where Eöüs was eke   85
With other three which Phaëton hade drawen
About the earthe till he became so seeke
As he fell doune where Neptune fand him fawen.

Bot to conclude the houre appointed came
Ye made you readie for to rinne the race   90
Ye bracke togither, and ranne out the same,
As Robin sayes, it had bene fil'd your face
It chanc'd ye were forerunne a prettie space
A mile or more, that keeped it so cleene
When all was done ye hade so evill [1] a grace   95
Ye stoll awaye and durst no more be seene.

Alias

Ye stoll awaye, and looked like Rob steene.

Remember of my protestation now
And thinke that love hath gar'd me take these paines
Fooles counsell whiles will helpe the wise [2] I trowe 100
Which reason makes me thus to breake [3] my braines
Great happe hath he whome others perils gaines
That moved me nou for to [4] repeate yone storie,

[1] Rait, *ill.*   [2] Orig., Rait, *will helpe wise men.*
[3] Orig., Rait, *is the cause that garrs me brake.*
[4] Rait, *mouit me for to. Nou* is inserted by James, and the two preceding changes are in his hand.

Proude Dares fall for all his might and meanes
105 Coulde no wayes teache you to bewarre of glorie
Nor yett woulde ye not call to memorie   •
What grounde ye gave to Christian Lindsay by it
For now she sayes which makes us all full sorie
Your craft to lie, with leave, now have I tried [1]
110 The proverbe sayes that mends is for misdeed
Cracke not againe no forder then the creede.

I William Mow at after supper lawing
With pen and drinke compil'd you this propine
I gatt it ended long before the dawing
115 Such pith hade Bacchus ou'r me God of wine:
Againe ye cumme if ye will essey me sine
To trie your horse that lost the other daye
We need not take no caire which of us tine
Since both our honours is long since awaye.[2]

[LII]

EX LUCANO LIBRO QUINTO [3]
Cæsaris an cursus vestræ sentire putatis
Damnum posse fugæ? et cœt.

If all the floodes amongs them wolde conclude
To staye there course from running in the sea
And by that meanes wolde thinke for to delude
The Oceane who shoulde impaired be
5 As they supposed, beleeving that if [4] he
Did lacke there floodes he wolde decrease him sell
Yett if we like the veritie to see [5]
It paires him nothing as I shall you tell

[1] Rait, *triit.*
[2] Rait, this stanza lacking.
[3] Poem crossed out in the MS., with the note, "This is alreadie printed."
Printed in *The Essayes of a Prentise*, with the title, *A Paraphrasticall Translation out of the Poete Lucane.* Printed in Rait, with no notice of its earlier appearance.
[4] Essayes, *if that.*   [5] Essayes, *wye;* Rait, *vie.*

For out of him they are augmented all
And most part creatt as you shall persave   10
For when the Sunne does sucke the vapours small
Furth of the sea which them containe and have
A part in winde, in wite and raine the leave
He rander does, which does augment the strands
Of Neptuns woll a cotte [1] sine they him weave   15
By hurling to him fast out ouer the lands.

When all is done, doe to him what they can
None can perceave that they doe swell him mair
I putt the cace then that they never rann
Yett noghthelesse that wolde him no wayes paire   20
What needes he then to compte it or to caire
Except there follie wolde the more be shawen
Since thogh they staye it harmes him not a haire
What gaine they thogh they hade there course withdrawen.

Then [2] even siclyke [3] thogh subjects doe conjure   25
For to rebell against there Prince and King
By leaving him allthogh they houpe to smuire
That grace wherewith God makes him for to raigne [4]
Thogh by his gifts he shewe him selfe benigne
To helpe there neede and make them therby gaine   30
Yett wante of them to him no harme [5] does bring
When they to rewe there follie shall be faine.

Then floodes runne on your wonted course of olde
Which God by Nature duelie hath provided
For thogh ye staye as I before have tolde   35
And cast a [6] doubt which God hath else decided
To be conjoined, by you to be devided
Ye kithe your spite yett does the deepe no skaith
For [7] better were in others eache confided
Ye floodes, thou deepe, which were your dueties baith.   40

---

[1] Essayes, *coate*.   [5] Essayes, *no harme to him.*
[2] Essayes, *So.*   [6] Essayes, *in;* Rait, *ane.*
[3] Orig., *such like.* Changed by James. [7] Essayes, Rait, *Farre.*
[4] Essayes, Rait, *ring.*

[LIII] [1]

SONG.   THE FIRST VERSES THAT EVER THE KING MADE [2]

Since thought is free, thinke what thou will
O troubled hart to ease thy paine
Thought unrevealed can do no evill [3]
Bot wordes past out, cummes [4] not againe
5   Be cairefull aye for to invent
The waye to gett thy owen intent.

To pleas [5] thy selfe with thy [6] concaite
And lett none knowe what thou does meane
Houpe aye at last, though it be late
10   To thy intent for to attaine
Thoght whiles [7] it brake forth in effect
Yet [8] aye lett witt thy will correct.

Since foole haste cumes [9] not greatest speede
I wolde thou shoulde learne for to knoaw [10]
15   How to make vertue of a neede
Since that necessitie hath no law
With patience then see thou attend
And houpe to vanquise in the end.

---

[1] First printed in Pinkerton's *Ancient Scotish Poems*, Lon., 1786, Vol. I, p. 177, from the MSS. of Sir Richard Maitland.   Printed in Calderwood's *History of the Kirk of Scotland*, Wodrow Soc., 1843, Vol. III, p. 784, from a copy in Calderwood's MS.

[2] *Song* is in Charles's hand, the rest of the title in Carey's.   Pink., *Sonet be King James VI* . . . (with summary of contents); Cald., *The King's verses when he was Fyfteene yeere old.*

[3] Pink., Cald., *ill.*

[4] Cald., *turne.*

[5] Orig., Pink., Cald., *play.*

[6] Pink. has *awin* after *thy.*

[7] Pink., *Lat quhillis;* Cald., *Whiles, lett.*

[8] Pink., *Bot;* Cald., *By.*

[9] Cald., *is.*

[10] Pink., Cald., *I wold thou shouldest learne to know.*

FRAGMENTA
[LIV]

AN EPITHALAMION UPON THE MARQUES OF HUNTLIES MARIAGE :[1]—

If ever I ô mightie Gods have done you service true
In setting furth [2] by painefull pen your glorious praises due
If one the forked hill I tredd, if ever I did preasse
To drinke of the [3] Pegasian spring, that flowes without re-
　leasse
If ever I on Pindus dwell'd, and from that sacred hill　　5
The eares of everie living thing did with your fame fullfill
Which by the trumpett of my verse I made for to resounde
From pole to pole through everie where of this immobile
　rounde
Then graunte to me who patrone am of Hymens triumphe
　here
That all your graces may upon this Hymens band appeare. 10
O sonne of Cytherea faire, and thou Thalasse withall
Graunte that this band may happelie to these coupled
　folkes befall
And ô Volumna prent a will into there coupled harts
Which may retaine that union aye, on ather of there parts
O Venus make them brooddie als for to produce with speede 15
Wherin they may revive againe a blest and happie seede
Vitunnus and Sentinus als [4] in happie tyme indue
The childe when as it is conceav'd, with life and senses true
O Prosa with Egeria joyn'd, and thou Lucina bright
Her dolours make into her birth, by your assisting, light : 20
O thou Levana doe with love and cairefulnes embrace
The babe when it is borne which shoulde extend there happie
　race
O Vagitanus playe thy part and safelie doe it keepe
From all misfortunes and mischance when as it first does
　weepe

---

[1] Printed in Rait, with the supplied title, *A Fragment of a Masque.*
[2] Rait, *out.*　　　　　[3] Rait, *yone.*　　　　　[4] Rait, *all.*

₂₅ O thou Cunina [1] cairefullie doe watche the cradle aye
Preserving it from sicknes or from harme in anie waye
Rumina, with Edusa, and Potina joyn'd, doe see
That when it sucking is or wained, the foode may whole-
some be
And also for there upbringing, O Statilinus caire
₃₀ That to there perfect age it may a happie waye prepare
And thou O Fortune to conclude, make these and all there
race
To be beloved of Gods and men, and thrive in everie cace.
If for my saike ye Gods above these graces will bestowe
Before these nuptiall dayes [2] sume signe to me for promise
show.

Mercurius

₃₅ I messager of Gods above am here unto you sent
To showe by proofe your tyme into there service well is
spent
For they have graunted your requeste and for a signe and
seale
Since they them selfs amongs you men doe no wayes haunte
nor [3] deale
They therfor have directed here to honour all this feast
₄₀ Faunes, Satyrs, Silvans, that approache there natures neare
at least
And as [4] for there conductour have they sent the whisler
Pan
Who thogh a God yett drawes he neare the nature of a man
With Naiades, Hamadryades, Nymphes of waters, woods,
and wells
To judge on everie sporte wherat there brethren with you
mells

---

[1] Orig., Rait, *Cumina.*
[2] Orig., Rait, *Before these nuptiall dayes be done sume signe for promise show.*
[3] Rait, *&.*   [4] Rait, *als.*

And as for me for my adieu, I drinke unto you here   45
The horne of Amalthœe, with lucke, with wealth and mirrie
   cheere.

Nymphes

We [1] are sent by Gods above with these our brethren deare
Who are prepared for glove, or ring, or anie sporte with
   speare
And we have broght for victours pryse this yellow garland
   rounde
Woven of our haire, with pearls therat, which we in fishes
   founde.   50
Then knights goe to, and make you for it, we can no further
   saye
Essaye you brethren, thogh I graunte, unused at such a
   playe.

Agrestis

Good Sirs the marvelous cumming here of these goode
   neighbours mine
Hath moved me for to come and see, this jollie feast and fine
Such allridge people in such a sort to cumme to plenished
   grounde   55
But anie fraye and guided by a man was never founde
Good faith before was never harde the like of my convoye
No since Deucaleons floode, I trowe ye call it the floode of
   Noë
Me thinke Saincte Marie gentles here makes for sume game
   and glee
Wa sume good Sir lenn me a speare, what racks essaye [2]
   and see.   60

The valliant actes, the workes of worthie fame
That bruite hath blowen abroade through everie whair
Of King and Court of Scotlands noble name
There Martiall games, and pastymes brave and faire

---

[1] Rait has *heir* after *We*.   [2] Rait, *to say.*

4

65 Sume does your Court, to Arthures court compaire
Sume sayes to Charles the magnes it may be peere
This bruit at last made wandering knights repaire
From forrane uncouthe lands and travell here
Fra they arrived they sent me soone to speare
70 If anie in your Court woulde them essaye
To runne at ring or prove sume games at warre
They three shall be defendours at the playe.
  Sirs thogh this language seeme both hard and haske
  Appardone new come strangers in a maske.[1]

[*Scholar*]

75　　O Gods above how I am ravish'd now
A heavenlie Goddesse is come doune I trowe
Our senses to delude : what ever she be
She peerles is as all men will agree
And therfor Sirs here am I sent before
80　As he who might by language best decore,
As schollers can, this doubt whom to the faire
Should appartaine, whome of ye harde declaire
And whome into at equall strife doe fall
Wealth, beautie, noble race, and vertues all
85　Eache one of these makes her a suitour here
And she is cume unto your Grace to speare
Whome to she should encline of all this rout
Among the rest Madame leave me not out.

Woman. 1

　　What meanes these kappit men ?　what can this be,
90　Is all this bussines that they make for me ?

The vertuous man. 4

The sacred state of marriage it was made
That two conjoyn'd a holie life might leade

---

[1] The sonnet is omitted in Rait.

Zanie. 5

Good even Sirs all, good faith I think it best
You quitte me this and take you all the rest.

L. G.[1] 1

If that ye please Madame to make me yours   95
My rent and friends shall serve you at all houres
God if my father. (*Sould.*[2] 2.) What a kalland is this
Place sillie man Madame I will not misse
To ware for you this hand and sworde of mine
A man of spirit his honour will not tine.   100

Scholler. 3

I can with pen your prayses due proclame
If that ye please accept of me Madame.

Vert.[3] 4

Your vertues rare Madame I doe respect
I promise trueth if that may take effect.

Sould. 1

If anie here hath skill of fense come prove   105
Three markett strockes before my onlie love.

L. G. 2

If that the morrowe [4] Madame chance to be faire
Please see two speedie grayhounds rinn a haire.

Schol. 3

If that ye please Madame a song to heare
I'l sett the toone, and make the chareshoh [5] cleare   110

---

[1] Rait, L[*andwart*] G[*entleman*].   [3] Rait, *Vert*[*uouse man*].
[2] Rait, S[*oldat*].   [4] Rait, *morne*.
[5] Probably intended for *chorus;* the MS. is obscure. Rait reads, *I sett
the toone & maid the aers lang eir.*

Sould. 2

I whome no bloodie battells coulde effraye
Am now become a simple womans praye,
Bot what? no woman bot a Goddesse bright
No shame to blinded be with suche a light.

L. G. 3

115   If friends or rent may serve my turne in this
I houpe to get this Ladie full of blisse.

[LV]

THE BEGINNING OF HIS M^{TIES} JURNEI TO DENMARKE; NEVER ENDED [1]

True is that saying us'd of olde amongs philosophes wise
That to eschue his destinie in no mans hands it lies
And thogh that they as ethnicks blinde on fortune laide the
    cause
And on the course and influence of starres and of there
    lawes,
5 Yett doe we Christians clearlie knowe that it is God alone
Who did before beginnings all, on wor*l*dlie [2] things dispone
Even he into his glorious and stedfast shining throne
Hath given to everie thing a tyme when as it must be done
That thogh this statelie heaven we see, the seas, and solide
    grounde
10 Must perish, and must changed be into a suddaine stounde
Yett not a worde of his decrees shall ever fall in vaine
Bot must be at that instant done, he did for it ordaine
And so as I have saide it does from Gods preordining flowe
The certaintie of destinies, and not of starres does growe
15 For they as simple creatures can no wayes guided be
Except by him that creatt them, then judge how like is he

---

[1] Title in the hand of Charles.   Printed in Rait, with the supplied title,
On his own Destiny.   [2] The *l* supplied by the editor.

That can not stande nor rule him selfe, to guide so manie
    things
Turne famous kingdomes upside doune, make and unmake
    there Kings
Thus Ethnicks fonde thogh wor*l*dlie wise, not knowing anie
    God
Did first invent that fortune and the starres did rule the rod 20
For like a blindman lacking light they wandered here and
    there
By guesse with groaping, stumbling oft, bot knewe[1] not how
    nor where
And since sume Christians on there stepps Cimmerians hath
    no shame
To take upon them to debaite and putt in proofe the same.
O [2] soft and faire, redounding Muse returne into thy waye 25
Thou chooses here to large a fielde, and toto far astraye
And worse then that, thou are to weake a Momus to be
    bolde
So manie learned men to impugne that this conjecture[3] holde.
Then to returne to destinies, how [4] none can them eschue
I may affirme that in my selfe, I proved it to be true   30
For I as being a King by birth, it seam'd my lott was made
Thaire to resyde quhaire god my charge & burthen on me
    laide [5]
And lacking parents, brethren, bairns or anie neare of kinn
In cace of death, or absence to supplie my place therin
And cheeflie in so kitle a land, where few remember can   35
For to have seene governing there a King that was a man
Yett [6] thogh through these occasions all, it was my settled
    minde
That I shoulde never on uncouthe coastes a harberie seeke
    to finde : ~

---

[1] Rait, *uist.*   [3] Rait, *to meet and.*

[2] Rait omits *O.*   [4] Orig., Rait, have *that* after *how.*

[5] In the MS. the line begins with the words *to gouverne,* added by James and then crossed through and the line left incomplete. The line in its present form appears in James's hand at the end of the poem, with a sign that it should be inserted above. Rait has *Into that cuntrey to be tyed quhaire my empire uas laide.*   [6] Orig., Rait, *And.*

[LVI]

This largenes and this breadth so long,/this highnes so
    profounde,
This bounded infinite, the masse/confused of all this
    rounde;
This Chaos lourde, I saye, which in/it selfe suche uproares
    wroght,
And sawe it[2] in one moment borne/in nothing made of
    noght,
5 The brooddie bodie was wherof/the essence pure divine,
And foure contending brethren ought/there birth to bor-
    rowe sine.
Now as to these foure elements,/these twinne sonnes ment
    by here,
Towitt, the subtle aire, the fire,/the earthe, and waters
    cleere,
Composed they are not, bot of them/is all composed and
    made,
10 That can into our senses fall,/or may be thought or saide:
Now[3] if there qualities do poure/there whole effects within
Eache part of everie bodie mixed,/and so to worke beginne;
Or whether that on everie part/there beings they confounde
And so of beings double twaine/one bodie doe compounde;
15 Even as within the bottome/deepe[4] of christall glasses
    cleene,
The wine with the Acheloian sucke[5]/for to be mix'd is seene:
Or even as meate which wholesome is,/and subtle liquour
    fine
Doe mixe them selfs within us for/to change in chilus sine.
This by experience may we see/into the stick that burnes,
20 Unto the heaven his native house/his fire full swift re-
    turnes,

[1] Printed in Rait, with the first half of the first line as title.
[2] Orig., Rait has *selfe* after *it*.
[3] Orig., *Whither;* Rait, *quhither.* Changed by Carey.
[4] Rait, *hou* [hollow]. [5] Rait, *Achelien sakke.*

His aire it flies in vanished smocke,/his earth in cendres
    falls,
His water crackes into his knotts,/and as for succour calls.
Like warre dothe holde our bod'[1] in peace,/whose earth
    her fleshe it bene,
Who does into her vitall spirits/her fire and aire contene,
Her water in her humours lies :/yet[2] thou can see no part 25
In all our humaine bodie, where/eache one by naturall art
Hath not his mightie vertues mix'd,/allthogh we plainlie
    see
That ather one or other of them/the cheefe commander be.
Into the masse of seething bloode/this clayie dregg and
    thicke,
Is blacke melancholie which sadd/does to the bottome
    sticke,   30
Composed of earthlie substance grosse ;/in bloode the aire
    abides,
Which pure into the mids doe[3] swimme ;/the humour in
    the sides
It is the colde and wattrie phlegme ;/this foame that light
    does flote
And holds the selfe aloft, it is/the burning cholere hote.
I meane not that eache element/into his handes[4] retaines 35
The sceptre of one bodie aye,/his tyme about he raignes
The subject making for to stoupe/unto his lawe and will,
And als oft as his King is changed,/he changeth nature
    still :
Even as without respect of wealth, /of bloode or noble race,
Each worthie citizen commandes/a certaine tyme and
    space,   40
In citties Democratick free,/that suddainlie appeare,
Through changing of there magistrate/a changing[5] face to
    beare :
For people lightlie agitate/with divers humours strange,
Chameleon like with manners of/there rulers doe they
    change.

[1] Orig., *bodie.*   [2] Orig., Rait, *yea.*
[3] Rait, *dois.*   [4] Rait, *hande.*   [5] Rait, *chaingit.*

45 Even so the element that in/the wine as cheefe doeth
    raigne,
Whiles makes it drie, whiles wacke,/whiles hoate and [1]
    colde againe
By there commixtions imperfect/or perfect in it plac'd
Enforcing it to change as well/of vertue as of taste :
So as by processe of the tyme/the verjusse bitter greene,
50 Sweete winne becummes, then stronger wine,/sine vinaigre
    it bene.
Now even as when a Prince or King/does over us so com-
    mande,
As underneath the yoake of law/he gars his greatnes stande ;
He rules [2] without suspicion, and/the common wealth
    enjoyes
Most happilie a quiet state/without tyrannique toyes :
55 Bot if that cruell Tyranne like/he never satiate be,
With his good subjects saickles bloode,/and if his sworde
    doe flie
To bloodie sharpe the scabert still,/his rage it will not spare
In end to turne his civill [3] land / in deserts wilde and
    bare.
The like falls out when as one of/the elements empires,
60 Ouer his three fellowes modestlie,/and not there wracke
    requires ;
And when as a proportion/affeirand joynes we see
The subject humours with the cheefe,/though they un-
    equall be :
The bod' [4] in being then abides/and als it dothe retaine,
The speciall draughts of all his forme/which outwardlie
    remaine.
65 Bot if that like unto that King/who barb'rous did desire
That all the cittizens of his/most mightie great empire,
Boore bot one craige that by that meanes/(ô crueltie) he
    might ;
By one greate blowe bereave the lives/of all the Romans
    quitt.

---

[1] Rait has *sum tymes* after *and*.
[2] Rait, *reades*.
[3] Rait, *cruill*.
[4] Orig., *bodie*.

[LVII]

THE BEGINNING OF M[R] DU BARTAS EDEN : —

Thou mightie God, that of the worlde the birth did make
    me see,
Unfolde her credle also now, her childehoode showe[1] to me :
And make my spirit to walke athort the turning florish'd
    wayes
Of savourie gardens, where into still crooked but anie stayes
Of rivers foure the courses quicke : declare me what offence 5
From Edens both, chas'd Adams selfe and seede for his pre-
    tense :
And tell who of immortall did him selfe an mortall make,
To bring from heaven the antidote to us which we did take.
Give thou me grace the storie of the church to sing aright,
And als the storie of the Kings ; and grante that by thy
    might   10
I guide the worlde unto[2] her grave, my purpose making leste[3]
Even from the first of Sabboths all unto the hinmest rest.
Well knowe I that this surgie sea is lacking marche or
    grounde,
Bot ô thou holie pilote greate will guide me safe and sounde,
Unto the haven of my desire, where droucked then I shall ; 15
Extoll thy mercies maniefolde and paye my vowes withall.
O sacred floure du lis whose youth does promise to us all,
That even thy famous laurells greene matche Alexanders
    shall ;
Since that for to obeye thy will I flie into the skies,
Convoye my course with loving eye, and helpe the faults rise 20
From my to blounted fruictles pen ; in Pampelone so sume
    daye
Maye thou winne home thy croune againe the which was
    reft awaye :
So of thy neighbours evermore maye thou the honour be,
The love of all thy subjects true, and foes to feare for the :

---

[1] Orig., *now*.   This and the next two changes are by James.
[2] Orig., *into*.   [3] Orig., *laste*.

₂₅ So never may the heaven against the showe his wrathefull
    face,
Bot the Eternall be thy arme, his Spirit thy guiding trace;
So with my shearing sworde in hande and fighting at thy side
May I ou'rclothed with bloode and stoure so boldlie by
    the bide,
As for to cleave the Spaignoll hoaste, or force sume seaged
    toune
₃₀ The combatt done for Virgill serve to publish thy renoune.
    God did not onlie (Soveraigne Prince) the whole command
    bestowe
On our forefather Adam of this earthe and all belowe
In making subject to his yoake the scalie swimming race
Who with there little fins doe cleave the frothie seas apace;
₃₅ And these that have no other holde bot horrour of deserts
And these that bricole through the vaste of aire that feathers
    partis:
Bot choosed him als an dwelling place which happie was and
    more,
With climat temperate and faire, the which the dentie Flore
With variant ameling paimented [1] of springing floures most
    sweete,
₄₀ Adorned with Pomones fruicts, and als with Zephyrs smells
    repleete:
Where God him selfe did lavell just the alles with his line,
Ou'rcover all the hills with trees, with harvest the vallies sine;
And with the sounde of thousand brookes adjourned the
    sweetest sleepe:
Made cabinets faire at proofe of Sunne which out his beames
    did keepe,
₄₅ He squar'd a garden, and als he did plante, cleange, and
    labour sine
The everliving fairenesse of an fertle orchard fine:
The sacred rivers courses als he parted here and there,
And with a thousand coulours peints the face of meddowes
    faire.

    [1] Orig., *Did payment with the aimeling faire.* Changed by Charles or
Carey.

APPENDIX I

I

"The confession of Mr John Hammilton the Jesuit, with his Maties confutation therof." [1]   In Latin.

II

"A letter of Sr Walter Lyndsayes with an answer therunto of his Maties." [2]   In English.   Lyndsay, who has recently become a Catholic, attacks the Kirk in a series of ten questions, which are answered by the King with great sharpness and credit.

III

[A SCHEME FOR A POEM [3]]

Within short space after the writting of my Sonnets and suites to the Gods, it chanced Iris to cume doune, as she uses to doe upon the ordinarie counsell dayes of the Gods; to the effect that if the Earthe, or Thetis, or the small Gods, Nymphs, or Satyrs of woodes or waters, have anie complainte or suite to be given in to the counsell of the Gods, that she may carie them to them.   Fra tyme I sawe her, I gave her my suite; she saide it was not lawfull to her to accept anie mortalls suite: my answer was that I desired her onlie to give it to the Muses, and that if they tooke not upon them to presente it to the Gods, I was content she should rive it.   Upon that she presented it to them, who joining Mercure with them, did as I looked for, and finding the Gods at the counsell delivered the bill unto them, thus far in rithme. [4]   After the reading wherof they sollisted there answer, as they who hade interest, in a few verse of ballet

---

[1] Fols. 61–63 b.   [2] Fols. 64–65.   [3] Fols. 65 b–67.
[4] Note in the margin, damaged by clipping: [U]rania in na[me] of the [fir]st did speake.

59

royall : there purpose ended and Jupiter readie to aske the votes,
Envie cummes in and oppones in tragicall verse ; the parties
being removed, Jupiter beginnes to take the votes, and first he
speares Apollos vote in ballet royall, who in the like verse showes
him selfe verrie favourable to the suite, and halfe partie : Pallas
raisonneth against him in the like verse.   In the meane tyme
Diana cumming in to the counsell house, foregathers the Muses in
the utter house, who desires her to be favourable to the suite, and
in two sonnetts describes her power over the witches, and her
hunting in the woodes ad captandam benevolentam.   Within
short space after her cumming in, Jupiter straikes a stroake,
and a midds betwixt Apollo and Pallas in heroicall verse, promis-
ing in his sentence that it shall be possible to me, or anie mortall
hereafter to attaine to that perfection, if having a good ingine
he will take all earnest paines and travells whill he obtaine unto
it.   This sentence he commands Mercure to bring doune unto
me : then I describe there glorious rising, and gladd parting from
other, in the like verse.   Then Mercurius according to Jupiters
command, letts this decreet slide of his wande in my bed, whill
I am sleeping.   To conclude all, I showe in a sonnett, how greate
a grace the Gods hath granted, exhorting all men as well as my
selfe, to spare no paines nor travells, to attaine to so great an
honour, seing no honour may be reaped without travell.

IV

"His Ma[ties] letter to M[r] du Bartas." [1]   In French.   Printed
in Rait.   The King praises the poetry of Du Bartas and urges
a visit to Scotland during the following summer (1587), as early
as May if possible.

V

[A LETTER TO CHANCELLOR MAITLAND] [2]

Being cleene exeemed from sleepe or anie will therof, even from
the tyme ye left me yesternight whill this daye at foure a clocke,
idlenes and silence of the night sturred up my Muse to travell
and speache ; and as our mindes remembers best on the last
object before going to sleepe, so my muse hade reddiest in memorie your translation of my verses that ye redd yesternight, and

[1] Fols. 67 b–68.   [2] Fol. 68 b.

therfor she begood to worke thereupon, as well to spurre you to end out that ye have begunne, as to encourage you to translate likewise hereafter such short poëms of mine, as shall be thought best written. Upon these conditions then, I send you this sonnet. Vide supra pag. 35 [p. 31, XXXIII].

VI

"His Maties letter to Mr du Plessis."[1] In French. Escript à Theobalds, Octobre, 1611. The King thanks du Plessis for the present of a book dedicated to him, but feels that there is no scriptural warrant and that the times are not ripe for exchanging the pen for the sword in the war against Antichrist.

VII

"His Maties letter to Mr du Moulin."[2] In French. Escript à Royston, 16 Dec., 1611. The King thanks du Moulin for honorable mention in his book and for his defense of the doctrines in the King's writings. He censures, however, his interpretation of passages from Cyprian, Chrysostom, and other authorities, and indicates seven points for alteration in his second book, *L'Accomplissement des Prophecies.*

VIII

Copy of a letter from Doctor (Jacopo Antonio) Marta to King James.[3] In Italian. Padua, Feb. 19, 1612.

IX

Copy of a letter written by Philip III of Spain to the " Presidentes de todos los Consejos."[4] In Spanish. Oct. 23, 1612.

X

Copy of the decree p'acing the *Controversia Anglicana de Potestate Regis et Pontificis,* by Martin Becanus, on the *Index Expurgatorius.*[5] In Latin. Jan. 3, 1613.

XI

Arguments respecting the validity of the papacy of Clement VIII.[6] In English.

[1] Fols. 69–70. [2] Fols. 71–76 b. [3] Fol. 77.
[4] Fol. 77 b. [5] Fols. 78–78 b. [6] Fols. 79–81 b.

APPENDIX II

I

Antithesis. [Following the song, "Since Thought is free."] [2]

> Since thought is thrall to thy ill will,
> O troubled heart, great is thy pain !
> Thought unreveeled may doe thee ill,
> But words weill past come weill again,
> 5   Be never carefull to invent
>   To gett thy owne, but God's intent.
>
> Play not thy self with thy conceate,
> For God knoweth all that thou doth meane.
> Hope without faith will bring thee late
> 10   To thy entent for to atteane.
>   And when it breakes furth in effect
>   Thy wylie witt God will correct.
>
> Since of fool-haste came never good speed,
> Pray God to give thee grace to know,
> 15   That vertue onlie forced by need,
> Serveth little thanks to the by law.
>   On God's will, then, see thou attend,
>   If thou would vanquishe in the end.

[1] Not in the Museum MS., and not included in *The Essayes of a Prentise* or *His Maiesties Poeticall Exercises*. All save *The Lorde Prayer* (IX) have appeared in print.

[2] Printed in Calderwood's *History of the Kirk of Scotland*, Wodrow Soc., 1843, Vol. III, p. 784, from a copy in Calderwood's MS.

II

His Majesties owne Sonnet. [On the defeat of the Spanish Armada.] [1]

The nations banded gainst the Lord of might
Prepar'd a force, and set them to the way:
Mars drest himself in such an awfull plight,
The like whereof was never seene they say:
They forward came in monstrous array,   5
Both Sea and land beset us every where:
Bragges threatned us a ruinous decay,
What came of that? the issue did declare.
The windes began to tosse them here and there,
The Seas begun in foming waves to swell: 10
The number that escap'd, it fell them faire:
The rest were swallowed up in gulfes of hell:
   But how were all these things miraculous done?
   God laught at them out of his heavenly throne.

III

[Epitaph on Chancellor Maitland] [2]

Thv passenger who spyst with gazeing eyes
This sad trophie [3] of death's triumphing dart,
Consider, when this ovtward tomb thv sees,
How rair a man leaves here his earthly pairt,

[1] Printed, with Maitland's Latin translation, at the end of *Ane Meditatioun* upon 1 Chronicles xv. 25–29, Edinburgh, 1589; in the second edition of this treatise, London, 1603; in the 1616 Folio, p. 89. The text follows the 1616 Folio.

[2] Inscribed on a marble tablet on the western wall of the ruined parish church of Haddington, Scotland, above the Lauderdale vault. Printed in the 1655 and later editions of Spottiswoode's *History of the Church of Scotland* (ed. 1841, Vol. II, p. 464). The text follows an exact copy of the original epitaph kindly supplied (after comparison with the printed version) by the Rev. W. Proudfoot, of Haddington. Variants in Spottiswoode are in part accounted for by the illegibility of his MS.

[3] Spot., *Trophy sad.*

5   His wisdome, and his vprightness of heart,
His piety, his practice in ovr state,
His pregnant wit well versed in every airt,[1]
As eqvally not all were in debate.[2]
Then jvstly hath his death brovght forth of late
10   A heavy grief to prince and svbjects all
Who virtve love, and vice to trvly hate,
Tho' viciovs men be joyfvl [3] at his fall;
    Bvt [4] for himself, most happie, doth he die,
    Tho' for his prince it most vnhappie be.

IV

The Dedication of the Booke [5]

Sonet

    Lo heere (my Sonne) a mirour vive and faire,
Which sheweth the shaddow of a worthy King.
Lo heere a Booke, a patterne doth you bring
Which ye should preasse to follow mair and maire.
5   This trustie friend, the trueth will never spaire,
But give a good advice unto you heare:
How it should be your chiefe and princely care,
To follow vertue, vice for to forbeare.
And in this Booke your lesson will ye leare,
10   For guiding of your people great and small.
Then (as ye ought) give an attentive eare,
And panse how ye these preceptes practise shall.
Your father bids you studie here and reede,
How to become a perfite King indeede.

---

[1] Spot., *His quick engine so versed in every art.*
[2] Spot., *As equals all were ever in debate.*
[3] Spot., *Rejoices.*
[4] Spot., *So.*
[5] Printed in the first edition, limited to seven copies, of the βασιλικόν Δῶρον, Edinburgh, 1599; not included in later editions. The text follows the reprint of the first edition, Roxburghe Club, Vol. 108.

V

The Argument [1]

[Sonnet to Prince Henry at the opening of the βασιλικόν Δῶρον.]

God gives not Kings the stile of Gods in vaine,
For on his Throne his Scepter doe they swey :
And as their subjects ought them to obey,
So Kings should feare and serve their God againe :
If then ye would enjoy a happie raigne,   5
Observe the Statutes of your heavenly King,
And from his Law, make all your Lawes to spring :
Since his Lieutenant here ye should remaine,
Reward the just, be stedfast, true and plaine,
Represse the proud, maintayning aye the right,   10
Walk alwayes so, as ever in his sight,
Who guardes the godly, plaguing the prophane :
   And so ye shall in Princely vertues shine,
   Resembling right your mightie King Divine.

VI

Two sets of verses made by the Kinge when he was at
Burley House, intertayned by the Marquis of Buckingham. [2]

The heavens that wept perpetually before,
Since we came hither, shewe theyr smyling cheere ;
This goodly howse it smiles and all this store
Of huge provisions smyles upon us here.
The buckes and stagges in full they seeme to smyle, 5
God send a smiling boy within a while.

---

[1] Printed in the first edition of the βασιλικόν Δῶρον, Edinburgh, 1599 ; in
later editions ; in the 1616 Folio, p. 137 ; frequently in histories and poetical
collections. The text follows the 1616 Folio.
[2] Printed from the MSS. of Miss Conway-Griffith, *Hist. MSS. Com. Reports*, V, p. 409.

VII

A Vow or Wishe for the felicitye and fertility of the owners of this howse.

If ever in the Aprill of my dayes
I sat upon Parnassus forked hill,
And there inflam'd with sacred fiery still
And there proclaim'd our great Apollo's prayse,
5   Graunt glistering Phoebus with thy golden rayes
My earnest suite, which to present thee here
Behold my * * of this blessed couple dere,
Whose vertues pure no tongue can duly blaze.
Thou by whose heate the trees in fruit abound,
10   Blesse them with fruite delitious, sweete and faire
That may succeede them in theyr vertues rare;
Firm plant theym in theyr naytive soyle and grounde.
    Thou Jove, that art the only god indeede,
    My prayer heare: sweete Jesus intercede.

VIII

[A Prayer, written on a blank page of a volume of Montaigne.] [1]

Here lyith I nakit, to the anatomie
Of my faill hairt, O humane deyitie
O tryst the almychtie, loyk the almychte woird
O put one me thy rob, as quhylum lord
5   Thou putist one myne, me in thy bloid beleiue
And in my souill, thy secreit law Ingrave.

[1] Printed in *Notes and Queries*, Ser. VI, Vol. X, p. 186, as an extract from the *Leeds Mercury*, Sept. 6, 1884. The copy of Montaigne was in the library of J. P. Collier, and the poem was printed at the time when his books were sold. The erratic spelling — e.g., *loyk* for *look*, *woird* for *word*, *belieue* for *belave* = *wash* — may be due to mistakes of the transcriber or the printer; it does not represent the King's usual orthography.

IX

The Lorde Prayer [1]

Oure michtie father that in heavin remanie
Thy noble name be sanctified alwayis
Thy kingdome come.   In earth thy will and ranie
Even as in heavins mot be obayed with prayse.
This day give us, our daylie bred and meat   5
Forgive us also our trespassis ay,
As we forgive the other small or great
Lord, in tentation lead us not we pray,
But us from evill delyver evermore :
For thyne is kingdome we do all record   10
Almichtie power and everlasting glore
For now and ay.   So mot it be ô Lord.

[1] From the MS. *Paraphrase of the Psalms*, British Museum, *Old Royal MSS.* 18 *B XVI.*   Above the prayer is the following note : "Lat this prayer be written with the psalmes other before or eftir."   The paraphrase printed in *Notes and Queries*, Ser. I, Vol. V, p. 195, and attributed to James, is entirely different and contains no internal evidence of his authorship.

NOTES

THE titles and contents of most of the pieces in the *Amatoria*, as well as *His Maties Jurnei* among the *Fragmenta*, indicate that they were written at the time of the King's marriage, an account of which is thus essential to an understanding of the poems. Though there were tentative proposals several years earlier (*Bowes' Correspondence*, Surtees Soc., October 7, 1580), negotiations for the marriage were first seriously undertaken in the summer of 1585, upon the arrival of envoys to suggest an alliance with one of the daughters of Frederick II of Denmark. The ambassadors were given encouragement, and in the autumn Peter Young, the King's tutor and master almoner, was sent to Denmark as the King's representative. Young was again in Denmark in the summers of 1586 and 1587 (Thorpe, *Cal. S. P. Sco.*, July 30, 1586 ; Aug. 13, 1587), but the negotiations dragged on till the spring of 1589. The reasons for this delay were partly no doubt the King's youth and the possibility of a marriage with the sister of Henry of Navarre, but chiefly Queen Elizabeth's opposition to this match or any other the King might make. As early as 1585 her envoy Wotton had almost prevented the reception of the Danish ambassadors. Later Elizabeth was said to favor the French princess, who was reported "olde and croked." (*Papers of the Master of Gray*, Bann. Club, p. 161.) In reality, as Melville remarks, her aim "was to stay him fra any mariage, as sche and hir consail had ever done and delt, baith with his mother and him self " (*Memoirs*, Bann. Club, p. 368). When the King finally reached his decision, "efter fyften dayes advysement and devot prayer" (*Ibid.*, p. 366), it was in opposition not only to Elizabeth, but to his chancellor, Maitland, who was under English influence.

69

On June 18, 1589, George Keith, the Earl Marshal, who
was chosen as the King's deputy, set sail with a large company to act in the preliminary ceremony and bring the
bride to Scotland, and on August 20 the marriage was performed. In the meantime, the King, who was at first reported a cool lover, had worked himself into a fever of impatient excitement. Messages flew back and forth across
the North Sea, entreaties from James that the Queen and her
company "come away in Scotland." (*Papers relative to the
Marriage of King James the Sixth*, Bann. Club, p. 18.)
James was alone at Craigmillar Castle, where he "culd not
sleip nor rest" (*Melville's Memoirs*, p. 370), "impatient
and sorrowful" at the delay. It is interesting to know that
the poems were thus the fruit of real passion, even though it
was for an 'unknown mistress.'

At last, on September 15, word reached Scotland that a
storm had scattered the Scottish fleet and forced the Queen
to take refuge at Opslo (now Christiania), on the coast of
Norway. After another month of waiting, the King found
further delay both dangerous and unbearable, and on the
night of October 22 stole secretly down to the quays of
Leith and set sail in quest of his bride. (Cf. Peter Young's
Ephemeride, in *Vitæ Quorundam . . . Virorum*, Th. Smith,
London, 1707.) The explanation of his romantic venture
appeared the next day in a letter to the Council (*Papers
relative to the Marriage*, p. 12 ff.), written with a colloquial
freedom rare in royal proclamations. He had resolved on
the voyage "upon the instant, yea very moment" the news
reached him, but had kept his decision from the Chancellor
lest the latter be accused of "leiding me by the nose." He
wished to prove himself no "barren stock," nor "irresolute
asse quha can do nathing of himselff." The government
during his absence was to be in the hands of the Duke of
Lennox, with the Earl of Bothwell second in power.

After a stormy passage, the King reached Norway October 28, and two weeks more of rough travel by sea and land
brought him to the Queen. The final ceremony took place
at Opslo, November 23. It was considered too late in the

season to return to Scotland. Instead the bridal party traversed some three hundred miles of Norwegian and Swedish forests, "throw manie woods and wildernes in confermed frost and snaw" (*Melville's Diary*, Bann. Club, p. 186), crossed the *Sund* to Elsinore, and spent the remainder of the winter at Kronberg and Copenhagen. "Drinking and driving ou'r" (Letter James to Lord Spynie, *Letters to James VI*, Bann. Club, p. xix) was varied by visits to Hemingsen, the theologian, and Brahe, the astronomer. On May 1, James and his sixteen-year-old Queen landed at Leith and were escorted in triumph to Holyrood.

As has been said, most of the poems in the *Amatoria* were written during this exciting period, either before or soon after the King's departure for Denmark. The exact dates of their composition, though indicated so far as possible in the notes following, are not so significant as the evidence of their sincerity and of their connection with an actual episode in the King's life.

I

In this instance the date is fixed by the fact that the news of the storm reached Scotland, September 15, 1589. The English poet Henry Constable, who was in Scotland at the time (cf. Introd., p. xxxvi), wrote a sonnet in answer, "To the King of Scots, upon occasion of a Sonnet the King wiote in complaint of a contrarie [wind] which hindred the arrival of the Queene out of Denmark." (*Diana: The Sonnets and Other Poems of Henry Constable*, ed. Hazlitt, London, 1859.) The first four lines are as follows : —

> "If I durst sigh still as I had begun,
> Or durst shed teares in such abundant store,
> You should have need to blame the sea no more,
> Nor call upon the wind as you have done."

II

4. *Cataplasme.* A plaster or poultice. Cf. Montgomerie, *Misc. Poems*, VI, l. 11 : —

> "No cataplasm can weill impesh that pest."

6. *Frie.* Here merely in the sense of *burn*, with none of its modern connotation. Cf. Montgomerie, *Misc. Poems,* XLVII, l. 10 : —

"Quhilk freats and fryis in furious flammis of fy[re.]"

7. *Sicker.* Here as an adverb, — firmly, securely

8. *Hoalit.* Pierced. A return to the King's original phrasing, as a means of preserving meter and alliteration.

12. *Pann.* Probably a shortened form of *panic.*

III

4. *Mease.* Allay, moderate.

IV

The sonnet, though differently developed, resembles that of Ronsard (*Œuvres,* ed. Marty-Laveaux, Vol. I, p. 17) beginning as follows : —

"Quand en naissant la Dame que j'adore
De ses beautez vint embellir les cieux,
Le fils de Rhée appella tous les Dieux,
Pour faire d'elle encore une Pandore."

9. *Sprung of Ferguse race.* According to the legendary genealogies of Boece and Buchanan, Fergus was the first King of Scotland.

V

6. *Daylie fascherie of my own affaires.* Even during James's stay in Denmark he was troubled by petty broils and rivalry among his followers. "Bot the company that wer with his Majestie," writes Sir James Melville (*Memoirs,* pp. 372–373), "held him in gret fascherie [perplexity, annoyance], to agre ther continuall stryf, pryd and partialites." The Earl Marshal and Chancellor Maitland quarreled for precedence; George Hume 'shot out' William Keith from his office as master of the wardrobe; and "at lenth the hail wair devydit into twa factions — the ane for the Erle Mar-

chall, and thother for the chanceler, wha was the starker, because the King tok his part."

VII

One should make no inference from the poem regarding the author's interest in the Scottish landscape. It is a line-for-line translation of a sonnet by Melin de Saint-Gelais (*Œuvres*, ed. 1873, Vol. I, p. 78), usually considered the earliest in the French language, and derived in turn from the Italian of Jacopo Sannazaro. Wyatt's sonnet on the same theme (*Poems*, ed. 1858, p. 12) is taken directly from the Italian. The closeness of James's version to the original may be seen by comparison with the sonnet of Saint-Gelais, which follows : —

> "Voyant ces monts de veue ainsi lointaine,
> Je les compare à mon long desplaisir :
> Haute est leur chef, et haut est mon désir,
> Leur pied est ferme, et ma foi est certaine.
>   D'eux maint ruisseau coule, et mainte fontaine :
> De mes deux yeux sortent pleurs à loisir ;
> De forts soupirs ne me puis dessaisir,
> Et de grands vents leur cime est toute plaine,
>   Mille troupeaux s'y promènent et paissent,
> Autant d'Amours se couvent et renaissent
> Dedans mon cœur, qui seul est leur pasture.
>   Ils sont sans fruict, mon bien n'est qu'aparence,
> Et d'eux a moy n'a qu'une différence,
> Qu'en eux la neige, en moy la flamme dure."

7. *Butt.* Without.

VIII

2. *Of brethren four which did this worlde compone.* The familiar medieval theory of the four elements and the four corresponding humors, with their relation to the 'complexions' of the human body, the ages of man, the seasons of the year, etc., was one of the King's favorite topics. It is

referred to again in *A Dreme on his Mistris*, ll. 60–78, and is the main theme of the translation from Du Bartas (LVI). See note on the last-mentioned poem, l. 25.

IX

7. *Since Lezardlike I feede upon her face.* Cf. Montgomerie, sonnet XXVI [*To the King*] : —

> "I am a lizard, fainest of his face,
> And not a snaik, with poyson him to byte."

Laing, in a note on the passage in Montgomerie, quotes Chester's *Love's Martyr* (Grosart, *Occ. Iss.*, Vol. VII, p. 114) : —

> "The Lizard is a kind of loving creature,
>
> .   .   .   .
>
> From dangerous beasts poore Man he doth defend :
> For being sleepy he all sence forsaketh ;
> The lizard bites him till the man awaketh."

9. *Marigolde.* Lat., *solsequium.* Cf. note, XVI, 60.

13–14. The syntactical peculiarity of the closing couplet — here a series of nouns recalling the figures used above, followed by a series of corresponding verbs — is a frequent device in English and Continental sonnets. In the second sonnet on Du Bartas (XXVII), where it occurs again, it is taken directly from the French original. Montgomerie uses it in sonnets I, IX, XXXIX (a translation from Ronsard), and LVIII, the last ending with the fantastic couplet : —

> "Revenge, revert, revive, revest, reveall,
> My hurt, my hairt, my hope, my hap, my heall."

Brotanek, in his study of Montgomerie (*Wiener Beiträge*, Vol. III, p. 76), gives other instances of the device, but confuses it with "underwriting," or the "reporting sonnet," where the closing words of each line are repeated in the line following.

XI

5. *Sponke.* Spark.

7. *With.* This is, I think, not the preposition, but the verb *withe*, in the sense of twist or curl.

7. *Wandling.* Nimbly. (Cf. *wannle* = agile, vigorous. — Jamieson's *Scottish Dictionary*.) It is possible, however, that the word is a formation from *wand* = twig or branch, in which case it would mean forking or branching.

8. *Kithe.* Show, make known.

1–8. The comparison, not a common one in Renaissance poetry, is employed in sonnet VI of Spenser's *Amoretti:* —

"The durefull Oake, whose sap is not yet dride,
Is long ere it conceive the kindling fyre;
But when it once doth burne, it doth divide
Great heat, and make his flames to heaven aspire.
So hard it is," etc.

Though the King's sonnets and Spenser's follow the same unusual rhyme-scheme, this is the only suggestion of imitation I have found in their writings.

XII

6. *That in inconstance thou art constant still.* This phrase and the preceding comparisons are recalled in a letter from Sir George Carey to Sir Robert Cecil, August 2, 1593 (*Cal. Hatfield MSS.*, Pt. IV. p. 346): "Our Scottish news sheweth Scotland not inconstant in inconstancy, removing the state thereof as the heavens that ever more do change, nor the King at this instant less subject to the loss of his liberty than when he was in ten years taken nine times by contrary factions, each time in danger of his life. . . ." Cecil soon after repeated the words in a letter to his Scottish agent Colville, as shown by the latter's reply (*Letters of Colville*, Bann. Club, p. 102, August 21, 1593): "That matter [Colville's plans] being partlie committed to Mr. Lok, and be reson of the constant inconstancy of our estate, as your honour rychtlie termes it, to be with good advys sett down."

Carey had no doubt seen the poem when he was in Scotland as an envoy in May, 1589 (Letter Earl of Derby to Earl of Shrewsbury, May 21, Nichols, *Progresses of Elizabeth*, Vol. III, p. 27).

XIII

The stanza of the poem is the so-called French octave, employed frequently by Dunbar, Montgomerie (*Misc. Poems*, I, VII, X, XXVII, XXXII, XXXIII, etc.), and other Scottish poets. Cf. note in *Burns's Poems*, ed. Henley and Henderson, Vol. I, p. 371. In the *Reulis and cautelis*, Ch. VIII, James speaks of it as *Ballat Royal*, a name probably suggested by its use in the French ballade. For its possible relation to the Spenserian sonnet and stanza, cf. Introd., p. li.

8. *Aimeled.* Here, as in LVII, 39, and often in Dunbar, it means merely colored or decorated. Cf. Dunbar, *The Goldin Terge*, l. 13 : —

"Ennammalit wes the feild with all cullouris."

10. *Dolent.* Mournful, dismal.

XIV

This is one of the eight poems first printed in *Lusus Regius*. In a note on the poem Rait remarks, with insufficient warrant, that the language indicates a period following the King's accession to the English throne. As a matter of fact, the piece is in phrasing and contents largely a patchwork from the love poems of Montgomerie.

The word *dier*, in the title, is not easily explained, save as a careless spelling or contraction of *dirige*, *dirgy*, *dirge* (Lat., *dirige* = direct, the first word of a penitential psalm in the church Service), or as a variant suggested by a wrong notion of the derivation. One of the earliest instances of its use in the title of a poem is *The Dregy of Dunbar maid to King James the Fyift being in Striuilling* (*Poems*, ed. Baildon, 1907, p. 6). The MS., however, indicates that the title of the present poem was added on the formation of the collection, at a time when the name and the genre had become popular.

8. *Raging Roland.* Among the unpublished poems of J. Stewart of Baldyness is *Ane Abbregement of Roland Furious translatit out of Aroist* [Ariosto], dedicated to the King. (MS. in the Advocates' Library.)

18. *By the halse.* Lit., by the neck ; in mingled suspense and expectation.

40. *Dwine.* Decline, pine away.

49. *All wemen are in overs.* *Overs*, the plural of the preposition used as a noun, is the word required by the meter, and might be taken to mean excesses or extremes. *Kynde*, deleted in the Bodl. MS., would make the line a septenarius, and justify the explanation of *overs* as overse or obverse. In either case the meaning would be much the same.

XVI

For the lady addressed and the date of composition, cf. note on the poem following. The description of violent changes of weather at sea was perhaps suggested by similar passages in the *Histoire de Jonas* of Du Bartas; but in graphic detail the French poet is much more successfully imitated in the well-known *The Calm* and *The Storm* of John Donne. In the adoption of *rhyme royal* for his complaint James follows his own counsel given in the *Reulis and cautelis*, where he speaks of "*Troilus* verse" as suited for "tragicall materis, complaintis, or testamentis."

21. *Rashing on the ray.* Flapping against the sail-yards. *Ray* (O.N., *rá*). Cf. Knox's *History, Works*, ed. Laing, 1864, Vol. I, p. 109 : "Our Schottish schippis war stayed, the sayles tackin from the rayes."

28. *Doe threaten mixing heavens with sea and earde.* Cf. Du Bartas, *Histoire de Jonas*, ll. 40–44 : —

> ". . . l'onde emmoncelee
> Lui jette en contr'echange une pluye salee.
> On diroit que le Ciel tombe dedans la mer ;
> Que la mer monte au Ciel."

Cf. also Burns's *Brigs of Ayr*, ll. 125–126 : —

"Then doun yell hurl (deil nor ye never rise !),
And dash the gumlie jaups up to the pouring skies."

51. *A chatton toome.* An empty setting. "The broadest part of a ring, wherein the stone is set."—COTGRAVE. James may have remembered the phrase from the inventories of his Royal Wardrobe and Jewel House (ed. T. Thomson, Edin., 1814, pp. 267–269), where in the year 1578 appear the items : "A chatton without ane emerald," "A chaton without a stane." Rings of this description were probably not rare in Scotland during the reigns of James and Mary.

52. *Volier.* A volary or bird-cage.

60. *Solsequium.* Lat. for marigold or sunflower. Cf. Montgomerie, *Misc. Poems*, XV, ll. 1–4 : —

"Lyk as the dum
Solsequium,
With cair ouercum,
And sorou, when the sun goes out of sight."

61. *Luckned.* Closed. From *lucken* = to lock.. There is a species of crowfoot known in Scotland as the *lucken gowan*.

XVII

"My Ladie Glammes," to whom the poem is addressed, was Anne, a daughter of Sir John Murray, later first Earl of Tullibardine, a companion of the King's childhood and later master of his household. That his daughter was the 'mistris' of the poem is established by two letters from Sir John Carey to Burleigh (*Cal. of Border Papers*, Vol. I, pp. 31, 34), referring to her marriage to Patrick Lyon, Lord Glamis, afterwards first Earl of Kinghorn. "The master of Glaymes," writes Carey, May 10, 1595, "had promised his nephew the Lord in marydge to Sesfordes sister, and now by the Earle Marres crossing of it, he is to marrye with fayre Mistris Anne Murrey, the Kinges mistris." A second letter, June 3, states that the King and Queen have gone to Stirling, and that "shortly the great marriage shall be solemnized at

Lythquo between young Lord Glaymes and the Kinges mistress." Lady Glamis survived her husband twelve years and died in Edinburgh, February 27, 1618.

While Carey's letters leave no doubt as to the Lady's identity, attention may be called to a reference to a similar affair of the King's in a letter of Dr. Toby Matthew, Bishop of Durham, giving an account of Bothwell's offers to Elizabeth just after the surprise of James in Holyrood (cf. note, XXVII) : "Nowe as your lordship is lik to heare of all these, and manie other particulers more at large, as the kinges affection to the Ladie Murton's daughter, and a strange letter writt to some suche effecte, with some good assurance taken to bring a greater estate there into their association and into her Majesties devocion. . . ." (*Cal. of Border Papers*, August 2, 1593.) In another letter, August 15, Matthew adds that "the kinges love that was spoken of, is as his lordeship saide, the Ladie Murtons fayre daughter, wherein is conteyned a mysterie not cleerly to me revealed." Oddly enough, Euphemia, one of the fifth Earl of Morton's daughters, became in 1586 the second wife of Sir Thomas Lyon of Baldukie, Master of Glamis, and might thus have been referred to as "the Ladie Glammes." She was one of seven fair sisters famous as " the pearls of Lockleven," and was much younger than the rough and elderly politician whom she married. Matthew's second letter goes on to say that the Queen's cleverness and her jealousy might lead her to connivance in the wild schemes of Bothwell.

If the *Dreame* and the *Complaint* preceding are connected, as they should be, with Anne Murray, it must be assumed that they were written before her marriage in 1595, though not long before, since even at that date she was scarcely more than a child. The titles were probably added much later. The placing of the poems in this period is made more likely by evidence, other than that of Matthew's letter, that the royal couple were at this time troubled by petty mutual jealousies. Colville (*Letters*, Bann. Club, p. 109) has extravagant tales of the King's suspicions of both Lennox and Bothwell. Ordinarily, and later, their relations were sufficiently amiable. We should have heard more of the affair with Lady Glamis if it had been other than a conventional, half literary, flirtation. Its chief interest is its evidence that the King was not at all times the cool, uncourtly, hunt-loving gentleman of contemporary descriptions.

Unfortunately the poems contain no internal evidence to complete the identification. According to Sir James Balfour Paul, Lord Lyon, who has kindly read the description of the tablet, ll. 170–240, there is nothing heraldic in the passage; the tablet, which was presumably in the shape of a locket, was merely engraved or enameled with fanciful symbolical devices common in the age in which the poem was written.

10–16. A parallel passage occurs in the *Chorus Venetus* at the end of the King's *Lepanto* (*Exercises at vacant houres*, 1591) : —

> " The God with golden wings through ports,
>   Of horne doth to me creepe,
> Who changes ofter shapes transformd
>   Then Proteus in the deepe."

11. *Ports of horne.* The twofold gates of the house of sleep, one of horn and one of ivory, described in the *Iliad*, Bk. XIX, ll. 362–367, and in the *Æneid*, Bk. VI, ll. 893–896.

31. *Flying horse and riding foule.* Periphrases for Pegasus, the winged horsed tamed by Minerva and given to the Muses.

61. *The humours four.* Cf. note, LVI, 25.

88. *Wedd.* A pledge or gage.

91. *Cust.* Preterit of *cast*, here meaning to set one's mind to, or ponder.

117. *The secret vertues* of the amethyst. Pliny (*Nat. Hist.*, lib. xxxvii, cap. 40) refers to the notion that the stone was a preventive of inebriety (whence the name, $\dot{a} + \mu\acute{e}\theta\upsilon\sigma\tau\sigma\varsigma$) and a charm against noxious spells. Its value to the soldier and hunter is stated more explicitly in Cardanus (*De Gemmis et Coloribus, Opera*, ed. 1663, Vol. III, p. 50): "Effecit sedatum, vigilantem. Ebrietatem reprimere . . . testan-

tur; ad pugnas quoque et venitiones utile esse; acuit ingenium, et somnum minuit, vapores enim à capite arcet." Cf. also the poem of Remy Belleau, *Les Amours et Nouveaux Eschanges des Pierres Precieuses* (*Œuvres*, ed. Marty-La-veaux, Vol. II, p. 165) : —

> " . . . en garde son porteur
> De jamais s'enivrer de ma douce liqueur.
>
> .   .   .   .
>
> Plus je vueil qu'elle rende agreable et gentil,
> Sobre, honeste, curtois, d'ésprit promt et subtil."

XVIII

In the *Reulis and cautelis*, Ch. VII, James quotes a six-line tetrameter stave of Montgomerie's, rhymed as in the present poem, with the comment : " In materis of love, use this kynde of verse, quhilk we call *Commoun* verse. . . . Lyke verse of ten feet [syllables], as this foirsaid is of aucht, ye may use lykewayis in love materis." Gascoigne, in his *Notes of Instruction* (*Elizabethan Critical Essays*, Vol. I, p. 54), calls the same stanza *ballade*.

James's sources for the animal lore of the poem, so far as it is not a matter of common observation, are suggested by his note on the *Phœnix* at the end of *The Essayes of a Prentise*, where he quotes Pliny's *Historia Naturalis*, and adds that he has helped himself also to "the Phœnix of Lactantius Firmianus, with Gesnerus de Avibus, & dyvers uthers." Cardanus, *De Animalibus* (*De Rerum Varietate*, lib. vii), would have supplied all that was not in Pliny; and the fifth and sixth 'Days' of Du Bartas are little more than Pliny turned into verse. Both versified natural history and satire on women are common enough types of poetry; but the mingling of the two in the present poem is, so far as the editor is aware, original with James.

3. *Marlions*. A variety of hawk.

5. *Mavises*. Thrushes.

6. *And lavrocks after Candlemasse to spring.* I find no authority for the exact date. In the Bodl. MS., *spring* is a substitution for *sing.*

10. *Gledds.* Kites, falcons.

11. *Kaes.* Jackdaws.

18. *Ounces.* Lynx (O. F., *l'once*). The loss of the initial letter is due to confusion with the article.

21. *Conns.* Squirrels.

27. *Remora.* Suckerfish. Cf. Spenser's *Worlds Vanitie,* ll. 108–109 : —

> "A little fish, that men called Remora,
> Which stopt her course, and held her by the heele."

28. *Sea horse.* Hippopotamus.

29. *Crevises.* Crayfish.

31. In medieval legend, mermaids and sirens were usually confused. Cf. Spenser, *Faërie Queene,* II, xii, st. 21 : —

> " Transform'd to fish, for their bold surquedry ;
>
> .   .   .   .
>
> To allure weake travellers whom gotten they did kill."

32. *As delphins loves all bairns.* Pliny (lib. x, cap. viii) tells of children carried on dolphins' backs and otherwise befriended.

34. *Mareswines.* Porpoises (Lat., *piscis porcus;* Mod. Fr., *marsouin*).

35. *Salmon.* In a letter to the Privy Council of Scotland, December 15, 1616, giving reasons for his projected visit in the next year, the King speaks of a "salmonlyke instinct of ours . . . to see our native soil and place of our birth and breeding."

36. *Selchs.* Seals.

36. *Rawnes,* roe. ˙ Cf. Pliny, lib. ix, cap. xv.

XIX

Since the seas still separated the lovers (cf. l. 5), the song must have been written before the King's departure for

Norway. The "long wished meeting," then, would refer merely to the one anticipated. Rait connects with the poem the following characteristically familiar letter from Queen Anne to the King (*Letters to King James the Sixth*, Bann. Club, p. xlv) : —

"Your Ma : letter was wellcume to me. I have bin as glad of the faire weather as your self; and the last part of your letter, you have guessed right that I would laugh — who wold not laugh — both at the persons and the subject, but more at so well a chosen Mercurie betweene Mars and Venus, and you knowe that women can hardly keepe counsell, I humbly desire your Mt. to tell me how it is possible that I should keepe this secret that have alreadie tolde it, and shall tell it to as manie as I speake with; if I were a poete I wold make a song of it, and sing it to the tune of Three fooles well mett."

The letter is undated, but the intimate style and the references to the weather and the English tune indicate that it was written long after their marriage. The editor of the *Letters* connects it plausibly with the incongruous match between the Earl of Nottingham, a gallant of seventy years, and Lady Margaret Stuart, September, 1603.

XX

3. *Leanders hart and Heros als.* Cf. a letter of W. Asheby, an English correspondent in Scotland, to Elizabeth (*Cal. S. P. Sco.*, October 23, 1589) : "The King's impatience for his love and lady hath so transported him in mind and body that he is about to commit himself, Leander like, to the waves of the ocean." It seems likely that the writer got his comparison from the song, in which case the latter must have been written prior to the King's departure.

29. *Whill envie called a naile.* If, as is likely, the poem was written before the King left Scotland, the obstacle in question may be connected with Queen Elizabeth and Maitland. Of their conduct during the spring of 1589, while the

marriage was still in debate, Sir James Melville writes as follows: "The Quen of Englandis answer was, not to mary in Denmark. Sche had credit with K. and princes of Navarre. . . . Upon this answer of England, our counsail wer convenit, and pratikit and intysed to vot, as the maist part of them did, against the marriage of Denmark. Whereat his Maieste tok sic a dispyt, as that he caused ane of his maist famylier servandis deall secretly with some of the deakens of the craftismen of Edenbrough, to mak a maner of mutinerie against the chanceler and consaill, boisting to slay the said chanceler, incaice the mariage with the K. of Denmarkis dochter wer hendrit or any langer delayed." — *Memoirs*, Bann. Club, p. 368.

XXI

The poem is quoted by T. F. Henderson, *Scottish Vernacular Literature*, p. 267, with the comment that it has "a certain semblance of dignity and grace . . . but the close is mean and tame; nor has the poem anything of the character of a sonnet." The final couplet, though here slightly improved by the King's change of *do his will* to *honoure him*, is spoiled for modern ears by the faulty rhyme. As a rule the attention to formal structure in the King's sonnets is one of their chief virtues.

4. *Bearded.* Used of a comet (*stella crinita*) with a train or tail.

6. *Rearding.* Roaring; applied especially to the noise of thunder. Cf. XLIII, 14.

XXII

Patrick Adamson (1537–1592) received his education in Scotland; but, like most Scottish scholars of the period, he spent several years abroad (1566–*c.* 1571). On his return he was granted, in 1572, a pension of £300 from the Crown (Calderwood, *History of the Kirk of Scotland*, Vol. III, p. 210), and was already in expectation of the Bishopric of St. Andrews (*Ibid.*, p. 206), to which he was finally appointed in 1576. On his promotion to this rich benefice, the poet Montgomerie remarked that he had often heard Adamson say, "The prophet wald mean this," but he never understood what the profit really meant till now. (Melville's *Diary*, Bann. Club, p. 45.)

Together with the Bishop of Glasgow, Robert Montgomerie, Adamson was made a kind of opening wedge for the establishment of episcopal church government in Scotland, and consequently a butt for the attacks of the reformers. He was soundly abused in verse by Robert Semple, and often greeted in the pulpit by the groans and hisses of the faithful. In 1582, on the victory of the Kirk Party, Adamson retired to his Castle of St. Andrews, where he lay according to Calderwood (Vol. V, p. 716) "like a tod in a hole" sick of a great "feditie" or swelling (for curing which a witch was later burned by the ministers). In 1590, Adamson was excommunicated by the Kirk, deserted by the King, and the income of his see turned over to the young Duke of Lennox. Whether deserved or not, this treatment is a rare instance of unfaithfulness on the part of the King to a former friend and servant.

Adamson's paraphrase of *Jobus*, in Latin hexameters, was written in Bourges in 1567–1568, but was not printed till his works were collected in *Patricii Adamsoni . . . Poemata Sacra*, London, 1619. The King's complimentary sonnet was also first printed in this collection.

1. *Bewes.* Boughs.

XXIII

The home of the famous Danish astronomer Tycho Brahe was on the small island of Hveen, in the sound between Elsinore and Copenhagen, where he had built a large observatory and castle called Uraniborg. Here James visited Brahe, March 20, 1590, and spent the day in learned discourse, — "de mobilitate præsertim, quam terræ Copernicus tribuit." (*Tychonis Brahei . . . vita*, Petro Gassendi, The Hague, ed. 1654, pp. 103–105.) In 1593 James sent the astronomer a thirty-year privilege for the circulation of his books in Scotland, and with it two sets of verses in Latin, which were published in Brahe's *Astronomiæ instauratæ Progymnasmata*, Prague, 1602. (Cf. E. Dreyer, *Tycho Brahe, a Picture of Scientific Life and Work in the Sixteenth Century*, Edinburgh, 1890, pp. 202–204.) The Latin verses are translations of the second sonnet printed here and of the hexastich following (XXIII, XXIV). The colophon in Brahe reads, "Jacobus Rex f. manuque propria scripsit"; but it is probable that the translations were by Maitland. Cf. *A Sonnet to Chanceller Maitlane*, XXXIII, and note.

XXIV

3. *Graithe.* Equipment, apparel.
11. *Looke.* For its use as a transitive verb, cf. App. II, VIII, 3. Cf. also *Bas. Dor.*, Roxb. Club, p. 12: "Look the Evangelists."

XXV

The translation in Brahe's *Instauratæ* is given in Irving (*Lives of the Scotish Poets*, Vol. II, p. 220) as follows: —

"Quàm temere est ausus Phaëton, vel præstat Apollo,
Qui regit iginomos æthere anhelus equos:
Plus Tycho: cuncta astra regis; tibi cedit Apollo;
Charus et Uraniæ es hospes, alumnus, amor."

XXVI

This poem was originally intended for Thomas Hudson's translation of Du Bartas's *Judith* (cf. Introd., p. xl), and was published with it in 1584, and again with Hudson's translation in the 1608 and later editions of Sylvester. The title was first supplied in the present collection and is clearly inappropriate; Hudson's English descent is referred to at the opening of the sonnet, and his modesty at the close.

1–3. The proper reading is that of the sonnet as first printed in Hudson: —

" Since ye immortal sisters nine hes left
    All other countries lying farre or neere
    To follow him who from them all you reft."

9. *Youre. His*, the reading in Hudson, is again preferable.
13. *Nor preasseth but to touche the laurell tree.* The line
refers to the motto on Hudson's title-page : —

"Ye learned, binde your browes with Laurer band :
    I prease but for to touch it with my hand,"

which is itself an adaptation of the last lines of Du Bartas's
L'Uranie.

XXVII

The poem is a close translation of a fantastic sonnet by
C. De Thouart, at the beginning of Du Bartas's *Seconde
Semaine.* Thouart's version, which follows, is in turn an
awkward variation of sonnet CXV in the *Olive* of Du
Bellay : —

"De quel ciel tires-tu ton scavoir incroyable ?
    Quel est le feu divin, qui t'inspire l'ardeur ?
    Quel oiseau pilles-tu pour trasser ton labeur ?
    Où cueilles tu les fleurs d'un livre immutable ?
Sainct, pur, seul, et orne (à nul qu'à toy semblable)
    Entendu, contemplé, leu et fleure par l'heur
    De ton rare scavoir, clairté, plume et odeur
    Au ciel, feu, air, et terre on te trouve admirable.
O grand Dieu qui entens du haut ciel ces chansons :
    Qui connois ton harpeur, ardeur, plume et fleurons
    Ne permets qu'il perisse en sa course imparfaite :
Toujours assez à temps son scavoir dans les Cieux
    Changera l'ame en Astre, et son ardeur en feux,
    Sa plume en Phœnix, et son corps en fleurette."

11. *Midrinke.* The word is a translation of *course im-
parfaite* in Thouart's sonnet. It is not given in *N.E.D.;*
but since *rink* was the usual Scottish word for the course in
a joust or tournament, *midrinke* may be explained as mid-
course or mid-career.

XXVIII

6. *Ponant.* The west. A formation from Lat. *ponere* after the analogy of Levant. Cf. Du Bartas, *Première Semaine, Second Jour.*, l. 397 : —

"De l'Aurore au Ponant, et du Ponant encore."

XXIX

The MS. of Fowler's translation of Petrarch, preserved in the Drummond Collection in the Edinburgh University Library, is described by Irving (*History of Scotish Poetry*, p. 464) as follows: "*The Trivmphs of the most famovs Poet Mr. Francis Petrarke, translated ovt of Italian into Inglish by Mr. Wm. Fouler, P. of Hauicke.* MS. fol. The dedication [to the wife of Chancellor Maitland] is dated at Edinburgh on the 17th of December, 1587. The King's sonnet is followed by other two, written by E. D. in praise of her friend the translator; and after three sonnets by R. Hudson, R. Cockburne, and T. Hudson, occurs a hexastich by A. Colville." R. Cockburne was Sir Richard Cockburne of Lethington, a nephew of Maitland, who received in April, 1591, the latter's office of Secretary of State. A. Colville was a son of Alexander Colville, Commendator of Culross, and succeeded to the title on his father's death in 1597 (*Letters of J. Colville*, Bann. Club, p. xii.) Both Cockburne and Colville, like Fowler, were at times correspondents in the English service.

13. *Love, chastness, deathe, and fame.* The themes of the first four of Petrarch's six *Trionfi.*

XXX

While there is no evidence that Sidney ever visited Scotland, there is good reason for believing that he and James were on friendly terms and that communication had passed between them. Sir Edward Wotton's letters of instruction on his departure for Scotland as ambassador were delivered to him by Sidney (*Cal. S. P. Sco.*, May 23, 1585), who may well have added such books and verse as he thought would please the King's taste. It was in the saddle bags of envoys that books and culture were generally carried into Scotland. James's favorite, the Master of Gray, was also a friend of Sidney. "He and I," writes Gray, "had that friendship, I must confess the truth, that moved me to desire so much my voyage to the Low Countries." (*Papers of Gray*, Bann. Club, November 6, 1587). Gray was a scholar, and no doubt strengthened his position at court by tales of the accomplishments of his poetical acquaintance in England. At the close of Sidney's last letter to Gray, from Nymwegen, May 17, 1586 (*Ibid.*, p. 78), there is a message to the King of more than conventional friendliness : "And which is the last, or rather the first point, hold me, I beseech you, in the gracious remembrance of your King, whom indeed I love."

In the Cambridge poems, James's sonnet is followed by a Latin translation and a hexastich, both by the King, together with translations from the hands of the Master of Gray, Maitland, Alexander Seaton, and Col. Ja. Halkerton (a leader of Gray's troops for the Low countries. — *Ibid.*, p. 78). The King's Latin sonnet is entitled, *In Philippi Sidnæi interitum Illustrissimi Scotorum Regis carmen;* it is reprinted, with the hexastich, in Irving's *Lives of the Scotish Poets*, Vol. II, p. 216.

7. *Mell.* Combine or mingle. (O.F., meller.)

XXXI

John Shaw was killed in defense of the King on the night of December 27, 1591, during the Earl of Bothwell's attack on James and Maitland in Holyrood Palace. The townspeople were roused and Bothwell forced to flee. "Yett he returned," writes Burel (*Diary*, December 28, 1591), "at the south syde of the Abbay, quher the said Earle and hes complices slew hes Maiesties maister stabler named Villiam Shaw, and ane with him naimed Mr. Peiter Shaw." Eight of Bothwell's fellows were caught and hanged next morning. "The 28 of December," continues Burel, "ye Kings Maiestie came to St. Geills Kirk, and there made ane oratione anent the fray made by Bothuell, and William Shaw's slauchter." The name William is probably due to a confusion with William Shaw, the King's master of works.

Montgomerie's *Epitaph of Johne and Patrik Shaues* (*Misc. Poems*, LVII) refers in lines 8–14 to the verses of the King :—

> "Then more praisuorthie Pelicans of Shawis
> Quhais saikles bluid wes for your souerane shed,
> Lo, blessit brether, both in honours bed !
> His sacred self your trumpet bravely blauis.
> By Castor and by Pollux, you may boste,
> Deid Shawis, ye live, suppose your lyfis be loste."

XXXIII

Sir John, first Baron Maitland of Thirlestane (*c.* 1545–1595) was a son of Sir Richard Maitland, now remembered chiefly for his collections of Scottish poetry, and a younger brother of William Maitland of Lethington, the secretary of Mary. Maitland was made Secretary of State (May 18, 1584), Vice Chancellor (May 31, 1586), and Chancellor (July 29, 1587). He was undoubtedly the most fortunately chosen of the King's Scottish councilors — not only 'the wisest man in Scotland,' in Burleigh's opinion — but one who was in sympathy with the King's middle course in politics and religion and could share his taste for books.

For the note which James sent to Maitland, together with the sonnet, cf. App. I, V. Maitland wrote Latin translations of the King's *Epitaphe on Sidney* (XXX), of his sonnet on the defeat of the Armada (App. II, II), and in all probability of the verses on Tycho Brahe (XXIV, XXV). These, with other of his poems in Latin and the vernacular, are printed with *The Poems of Sir Richard Maitland*, Bann. Club, 1830, pp. 120–143. The pieces in Scottish dialect are vigorous political satires, written as early as 1571–1572.

1. *If he who valliant*, etc. An allusion to Alexander's conquest of the world during the twelve years of his reign.

13. *Leide.* Language.

Olet lucernam, etc. The King probably had in mind Demosthenes' retort to Pythias when told that his arguments smelt of the lamp (ἐλλυχνίων ὄζειν). Demosthenes' answer as given in Plutarch (*Demosthenes,* vii) was to the effect that his lamp witnessed more commendable occupations than those of Pythias.

XXXIV

For Montgomerie's relations with the King, and the date of his death, cf. Introd., Ch. II.

2. *Castalian band.* The name adopted by the group of poets in the Scottish Court. Cf. Montgomerie's *Sonnet to R. Hudson* (XXV, l. 1) : —

"My best belouit brother of the band."

Cf. also Dempster's account of Montgomerie (*Hist. Eccles. Gent. Scot.,* Bann. Club, p. 496 : ". . . regi carrissimus Jacobo, qui poeticen mirifice eo ævo amplexabatur, quique poetas claros sodales suos vulgo vocari voluit. . . ."

XXXV

10. *Tirrar.* One who tears or strips.

XXXVI

The name *ænigme* and the form are both taken from the French (*e.g.* the poem entitled *Enigme,* Saint-Gelais, *Poésies,* Vol. I, p. 70). Montgomerie has a similar riddle on his lawyer, M. J. Sharpe (sonnet XXIII), and another on *His Maistres Name* (sonnet XLVI). This supports the presumption that the poem was written while the King was still in Scotland. The date is of especial interest, for in the sonnet the King is almost certainly emulating some earlier treatment of the familiar theme. One would like to believe that 2 *Henry IV* had been played in Scotland during one of the early visits of English actors and the King stirred by the beautiful apostrophe at the beginning of

Act III. This, however, is supported merely by the verbal similarity of the two passages; James may have derived his idea from Sidney's sonnet (*Astrophel and Stella*, xxxix), or more likely from some classical source such as Seneca's *Hercules Furens*, ll. 1065–1081, or the *Orphic Hymn to Sleep*. (For the sources of English poems on the subject, cf. A. S. Cook, *Mod. Lang. Notes*, Vol. IV, p. 466; Vol. V, p. 11.)

XXXVII

Francis Stewart Hepburn (*c.* 1563–1624) was the sixth Earl of Bothwell, a nephew of Mary's Bothwell, and an illegitimate grandson of James V. His raids and surprises made him, in the phrase of the ministers (Calderwood, Vol. V, p. 256), "a sanctified plague" to the King, and were so frequent that it is not easy to decide to which one the present poem and the two following refer. The circumstances, however, best fit what the King himself calls "Bothwell's surprysing of my person" (*Letters of James to Eliz.*, Camd. Soc., p. 88), July 24, 1593. Bothwell and John Colville, the Earl's companion and an agent in the employ of Burleigh, were concealed in the early morning behind the arras in the King's antechamber, and the door leading to the Queen's room was locked lest the King escape. "He [Bothwell] had a drawen suerd in his hand," writes Melville (*Memoirs*, Bann. Club, p. 414), "and Mester Jhon Colville another. His Majesties claise wer louse, and his hose not knet up; yet he was in nawayes astonishit bot began calling them false traitours, bidding them stryk gif they durst." Bowes gives similar testimony regarding the King's courage and volubility (Tytler, *Hist. of Scot.*, Vol. IX, p. 89). Bothwell kneeled melodramatically and presented his sword. By this time Lennox, Atholl, and others were in the room and an Edinburgh rabble in the palace-yard. In the end Bothwell forced James to give him a commission of pardon, and rode off leaving the King practically a prisoner in the palace.

On the 10th of August, the Earl, now that he was in

power, consented to stand trial for treasonable practices, alleged to have been committed at the time of the King's marriage. He was accused of bargaining with the wizard Graham for a poison "made of adders skynnes, tode skynnes, and the hipomanes in the forehead of a yong fole, all which being joined by there arte together, should be such a poison as being laid where the kinge should come, so as yt might dropp uppon his head, yt wold be a poison of such vehemencye, as should have presently cut him off. Another maner device for his destruction was this — to make his picture of waxe mingled with certen other thinges, which should have consumed and melted awaye in tyme, meaning the kinge should consume as it did. A third mean to cut him off was — he should be enchanted to remayne in Denmarke." — Letter from Carey to Burleigh, *Cal. of Border Papers*, August 12, 1593. Neither the quality of the evidence nor the fact that James was still alive and back in Scotland had much to do with Bothwell's acquittal.

The morning after the trial, August 11, James attempted to escape to Falkland, but was discovered and stopped. Again, with the help of the English envoy Bowes, an agreement was patched up by which James consented to the pardon of Bothwell and the retirement of Maitland, Hume, and Glamis until the Parliament at Stirling a month later. For James, as he explained in a message to Elizabeth (*Letters*, Camd. Soc., p. 89), this was the mere "shaddow of a promeis . . . forcit not onlie for my owin safetie but also for the safetie of my quhole countrey in me" — simply a truce, as every one concerned understood. Before the parliament assembled, James's power was strengthened and Bothwell forced into an alliance with the Catholic party, — a false step, which caused his Kirk supporters to 'start and wonder' and astonished that devout Protestant and secret ally, the Queen of England. In November, Bothwell was given fifteen days to leave the kingdom and was forced to seek temporary refuge across the Border.

The three sonnets relate to this sequence of events and indicate the King's feelings and policy following his capture.

The "coloured knaves" and "monstrous foules" (XXXVIII, 5, 12) are Bothwell and his confederates. The complaints against Justice in XXXIX probably refer specifically to Bothwell's acquittal.

The form of the sonnet imitates the debates of Danger, Courage, and other abstractions in Montgomerie's *The Cherrie and the Slae.* Cf. ll. 393–402 : —

> "Quhat can thou losse, quhen honour lyvis?
> Renowne thy vertew ay reuyuis,
>   Gif valiauntlie thou end:"
> Quod Danger, "Hulie, friend, tak heid;
> Vntymous spurring spillis the steid:
>   Tak tent quhat ye pretend.
> Thocht Courage counsell thee to clim,
>   Bewar thou kep na skaith:
> Haif thou na help bot Hope and him?
>   They may beguyle the baith."

1. *Faschious.* Troublesome, vexatious. Cf. *Bas. Dor.,* Roxburghe Club, p. 125: "faschious thoughts on their affaires."

11. *Kithe.* Show, make known.

XXXVIII

3. *Farde.* A paint for the face. *Fained farde* was a conventional phrase for flattery or slander. Cf. *Mirrour for Magistrates, Lochrinus,* st. xxvii : —

> " Though yee coloure all with coate of ryght,
>   No fayned fard deceaues or dimmes his sight."

14. *Resave.* Receive.

XXXIX

With this poem should, I think, be connected sonnets VI and VII of Montgomerie, who at this time seems to have echoed from his retirement all the verses of the King that reached him. The second at least may be dated in this period by the reference in line 13 to "thir bluidy sarks," carried through Edinburgh, July 23, 1593, by women whose sons and husbands had been slaughtered by the Laird of Johnstone (Calderwood, *Hist. of the Kirk*, Vol. V, p. 256.)

2. *Fleemed.* From *fleme*, to put to flight.

8. *Speare.* Ask.

14. *Meschant.* Wicked (Fr., *meschant*).

XL

As indicated in the footnote, this and the three following sonnets are printed in *The Essayes of a Prentise* and crossed out in the MS. They are of slight interest and are reprinted merely to present the MS. completely.

XLI

8. *Windowes.* Eyes. Mercury lulled Argus to sleep by the story of Pan and Syrinx.

XLIII

9. *Thy greatest thunders.* Explained by a note in *The Essayes of a Prentise:* "Jupiter (as the Poets feinyeis) had two thunders, whereof he sent the greatest upon the Gyants, who contemned him."

11. *Semele.* James's note (*Ibid.*): "Mother of Bacchus, who being deceived by Juno, made Jupiter come to her in his least thunder, which nevertheless consumde her."

14. *Rearde.* Roar, as of cannon or thunder.

XLV

The evidence of the sonnet regarding Montgomerie's convivial habits requires no comment. For the date of his death, cf. Introd., p. xxxii.

3. *Twise borne boye.* An allusion to the untimely birth of Bacchus on the appearance of Jupiter to Semele in his least thunder. Cf. note, XLIII, 10.

4. *Wight.* Strong, powerful.

8. *Warde.* Rait, *uarrd;* glossed, *worsted.* The sense of the passage is that since Bacchus has overcome the master poet, lesser writers should cease to strive against him.

14. *Render.* Rait, *rander;* glossed, *talk idly.* But here, as in LIV, 14, it means surrender, give up.

XLVI

For the King's views of versification, as revealed in the poem, cf. Introd. p. lxxxix.

12. *Wayne.* There is a play on the words *wain* and *vein.*

13. *The mettalls.* Cf. variant, *your mettalls.* In 1613 James granted to Alexander the right of working a silver mine near Linlithgow, later abandoned as unprofitable (*Earl of Stirling's Register of Royal Letters*, Introd., p. ix).

XLVII

It is perhaps open to question whether the date 1616 in the title is old style or new, or has not already been set forward by mistake. In the years 1615–1617 the only severe cold mentioned by Stowe was the famous frost of 1615, when it began to snow January 17 and "continued freezing and snowing . . . untill the 14th of February at noon." James was at Newmarket in February of both this year and the one following. In Drummond (*Works*, ed. 1711, p. 14), the sonnet, including the title, corresponds almost exactly to its form as now printed. It was sent to Drummond in a letter from Alexander, printed with it. "I have sent you here," writes Alexander, "a Sonnet, which the King made the last Week, moved by the Roughness of the Season, as you may perceive by his Allusion to *Saturn* and *Janus* Meeting. This forced the Other from me." Alexander's verses may be quoted as a sample of the conventional flattery which was heaped on the King as prince and poet : —

> " When Britain's Monarch, in true Greatness great,
> His Council's Counsel, did Things past unfold,
> He (eminent in Knowledge as in State)
> What might occurr oraculously told ;

And when, far rais'd from this Terrestrial Round,
He numbrous Notes with measur'd Fury frames,
Each Accent weigh'd, no Jarr in Sense, or Sound.
He Phœbus seems, his Lines Castalian Streams,
This Worth (though much we owe) doth more extort;
All Honour should, but it constrains to Love,
While ravish'd still above the vulgar Sort
He Prince, or Poet, more than Man doth prove:
   But all his due who can afford him then,
   A God of Poets, and a King of Men."

2. *Band.* Bond. *Baleful band* = quarrel.

XLVIII

This sonnet may be connected with the one following
by the fact that both are in the hand of Prince Charles, and
by their difference in theme and superiority in finish and
dignity to the other poems of the collection. The departure
from the King's usual rhyme-scheme, in the second sonnet,
may indeed raise a question as to its authorship. But it
appears in a MS. which now contains no blank spaces, and in
which poems both before and after are corrected in the King's
hand. The broad Scots dialect, the alliteration, the so-
norousness of the verse, are all marked traits of the King's
style at its best, and make it advisable, in the absence of
other evidence, to accept the contemporary ascription.

2. *Thole.* Endure.

3. *Golden Tagus.* Celebrated in classical poetry for its
glittering sands. Cf. Lucan, *De Bello Civili*, Bk. vii, l.
755: —

   " . . . quidquid Tagus expuit auri."

4. This line reappears with but slight changes in a sonnet
among the *Poeticall Essayes of Alexander Craige, Scotobri-
tane*, London, 1604, p. 31 (Hunterian Club reprint). On
p. 18 of his *Recreations* (Edinburgh, 1609), is another
sonnet beginning, —

   " Fair famous Ile where Zoroastres reigned,"

7

— and imitative throughout of James's sonnet numbered
XLIX. Craige's *Essayes* are dedicated to the King, from
whom in 1605 he received a pension of four hundred
pounds Scots.

5. *Ladon*. "Pamela and Philoclea . . . resolved to beg
Zelmanes company and to go, while the heat of the day
lasted, to bathe themselves, as the Arcadian nymphs often
do, in the River Ladon, which of all the rivers of Greece had
the price for excellent pureness and sweetness." (Sir
Philip Sidney, *Arcadia*, bk. ii.)

XLIX

A clue to the date of the poem and the identity of the
lady referred to is given by its close resemblance to a sonnet
written by Sir David Murray of Gorty, Keeper of the
Privy Purse to Prince Henry, and published with *The
Tragicall Death of Sophonisba*, London, 1611 : —

"Sonnet on the death of the Lady Cicely Weems, Lady
of Tillebarne."

"Faire Cicil's losse, be thou my sable song,
Not that for which proud Rome and Carthage strave
But thine more famous, whom ago not long
Untimely death intomb'd so soon in grave.
Dear sacred Lady, let thy ghost receive
These dying accents of my mourning quill,
The sweetest-smelling incense that I have,
With sighs and teares upon thy hearse to spill.
To thee (deare Saint) I consecrate ay still
These sad oblations of my mirthlesse mind,
Who while thou breath'd, this wondring world did fill
With thy perfections, Phœnix of thy kind :
From out whose ashes hence I prophecie,
Shall never such another Phœnix flie."
— Bann. Club edition, 1823.

Lady Cicely or Cecilia was the eldest daughter of Sir John
Wemyss, and was married to William Murray, who on his

father's death in 1613 became the second Earl of Tullibard-ine. The contract for this marriage is dated October 30, 1599 (*Scots Peerage*, Vol. I, p. 471), and since Murray was married a second time — to Dorothea, daughter of the Earl of Atholl — in September, 1604, the death of his first wife must have occurred before the close of 1603. The King's sonnet was presumably written not long after, as also the Cœlia and Sophonisba poems of Sir David Murray, which may reasonably be connected with the death of his cousin's wife. Lady Cicely, it should be added, was sister-in-law of the Lady Glamis of the King's earlier poems.

1. *Agathocles*. Despot of Syracuse, in Sicily (367–290 B.C.).

1. *Rang*. Reigned. Cf. *Essayes of a Prentise, Lucanus Lib. Quinto*, l. 28 : —

" That grace, wherewith God maks him for to ring."

3. *Bangsters* [MS. bāgsters]. Swash-bucklers, bullies.

10. *Farelies*. Marvels, wonders. James puns on the same word in his remarks on the speech of Dr. James Fairlie, one of the orators in the disputations at Stirling, July 19, 1617, on the occasion of the King's visit : "The Defender is justly called Fairlie, his thesis had some fair lies in it, and he sustained them very fairly, with many fair lies given to the Oppugners." (Nichols, *Progresses of James*, Vol. III, p. 309.)

L

The sonnet bears a close resemblance to Montgomerie's *Complaint of his Nativitie* (*Misc. Poems*, IV), a poem of seven stanzas beginning as follows : —

"Since that the Hevins are hinderers of my hap,
    And all the starris so strange against me stand,
    Quhy kild not Jove me with his thunder clap,
    Hou soon the midwyfe held me in hir hand?"

Montgomerie's verses are a complaint to the King on the withdrawal of patronage, and it is possible therefore that the imitation may be attributed to him. In any case the original source is a sonnet in Ronsard's *Amours* (ed. Marty-Laveaux, Vol. I, p. 28) : —

> "Quel sort malin, quel astre me fit estre
> Jeune et si fol, et de malheur si plein ?
> Quel destin fit que toujours je me plain
> De la rigueur d'un trop rigoureux maistre ?
> Quelle des Sœurs à l'heure de mon estre
> Pour mon malheur noircit mon fil humain : " etc.

6. *Spean'd.* Weaned. (Cf. *spean* = spoon.) Cf. Melville's *Diary*, Bann. Club, p. 180 : "The bairn . . . seemed of a fyne sanguine constitution, till a quarter efter he was speaned."

13. *Marcellus.* A reference, not to the Roman Consul of that name, who underwent no serious tribulations, but to Marcellus I, who was elected Pope in the year 308, and died in 309. According to a legendary *Passio Marcelli*, he suffered persecution and was condemned to work as a slave.

LI

The poem shows clearly the extent to which Alexander Montgomerie, "the Master poët," and his fellows of the Castalian band were boon companions of the King's youth. The crossing out of the poem in the MS. may indeed indicate that the King hesitated to publish so complete a revelation of his early friends and pleasures, or else considered its facetious tone out of keeping with his royal dignity. The quotation of the tenth stanza in the *Reulis and cautelis* proves that the piece was written before 1585.

13. *Olde crucked Robert.* Robert Hudson, one of the four brothers who were musicians of the Chapel Royal (cf. Introd., p. xxxix). His lameness seems to have suggested to Montgomerie a comparison with Vulcan, the lame blacksmith of mythology : —

"My best belouit brother of the band,
  I grein to sie the sillie smiddy smeik."
                    — Sonnet XXV, *To R. Hudsone*.

"The smeikie smeithis cairs not his passit trauel."
                    — Sonnet XXX.

2. *Sanders*.   A familiar abbreviation of Alexander.

13. *Makes of you the haire*.   Gives you no attention, 'does not care a hair.'   Cf. LII, 23.

14. *Elfegett Polward*.   The adjective is suggested by l. 282 of Montgomerie's *Flyting* with Polwart, quoted later in the *Reulis and cautelis :* —

"There ane elf, on ane ape, ane unsell begat."

Sir Patrick Hume of Polwarth (d. 1609), the opponent in the *Flyting,* was at one time master of the household and a gentleman of the bed-chamber to King James, and later a warden of the marches.   He was the author of *The Promine, conteyning the maner, place, and time, of the maist Illuster King James the Sext his first passing to the feildis: directit to his hieness: Be P. H. familiar servitour to his Maiestie,* Edinburgh, 1580.   (Reprint in Pinkerton's *Anc. Pop. Poetry,* Edin., 1822.)   The poem is a piece of conventional extravagance of no biographical value.

16. *To winne the chimnay nuike*.   Another reference to the *Flyting*, in which the aim of the contest was to drive the opponent from his seat in the chimney corner.   Cf. Montgomerie, sonnet XXVII : —

"Vhose Highnes laughed som tym for to look
  Hou I chaist Polwart from the chimney [nook]."

18. *Rype*.   To clear out, or clean.   Cf. "rype the ribs [of a grate]."   (Jamieson's *Scottish Dictionary*.)

25. *Cracking crouslie*.   Talking or boasting boldly.   Cf. Burns, *Twa Dogs*, l. 135 : —

"The cantie auld folks cracking crouse."

25. *Broune.* Rait explains as *brownie*, and says it is here "used in the somewhat unusual sense of the inspiring genius of a poet." It seems more probable that it refers to the color of the horse.

29. *Yaulde and wight.* Supple and strong. *Yaulde* seems to be an adj. from the pp. of *yield*.

31. *Beleeve.* At once, soon.

35. *As Dares did.* The story of the contest between Dares and Entellus is from the *Æneid*, Bk. V, ll. 362–484. James, no doubt, wrote from memory of the original. The closest verbal resemblance to Gawain Douglas's translation is in lines 40–46. Cf. Douglas, S. T. Soc., Bk. V., Ch. vii : —

> "Son of the Goddes, gyf na man wil rys
> Ne dar hym self adventure in batelle
> Quhy stand I thus? quhou lang efferis me duell?
> Cummand me leid away the pryce al fre."

35. *Ou'rhye.* Domineer over, outboast.

71. *Feade.* Feud, enmity.

73–80. The stanza is quoted in the *Reulis and cautelis* as an example of verse "for any heich grave subjectis, specially drawin out of learnit authouris . . . callit *Ballat Royal.*" In the quotation, *ye* (l. 73) reads *he*, and *was* (l. 80) reads *Fell*.

72. *No Latt.* Not stop, not be given up.

73. *Grien'd.* Grieved, longed.

78. *Gettie.* Black as jet.

80. *Which turned into a floure.* An alteration of the legend for exigencies of rhyme. Tithonus was changed into a cricket.

88. *Fawen.* Fallen.

92. *It had bene fil'd your face.* Your face had been defiled. A French construction, no doubt less awkward in James's time than to-day. Rait calls attention to the similar accident to Nisus in the race preceding the boxing match (*Æneid*, Bk. V).

97. *Rob steene.* A clever verse satire against Chancellor Maitland, written in 1591 and entitled *Rob Stene's Dreme,*

was published by the Maitland Club in 1836. Mr. Geo. Neilson (*Sco. Hist. Rev.*, Vol. II, p. 253, and cf. p. 280) has shown that there was actually a person of this name, who received a salary of £72 from the crown in the year 1587–1588, was later a schoolmaster of Edinburgh, contributed Latin verses to *The Muses Welcome* on the King's return to Scotland in 1617, and died in February, 1618. Neilson concludes that the author of the satire was this Edinburgh schoolmaster.

While space is lacking to consider this view at length, the connection of the name with Montgomerie should be indicated. In the *Flyting*, l. 660, Polwart applies the epithet directly to his opponent : —

"Rob Stevin thou raues, fotgetting whom thou matches."

It occurs again, according to Neilson, in the unpublished poems of J. Stewart of Baldyness, dedicated to the King, where a set of verses, in which the last words of each line are repeated in the first of the next, is spoken of as "rym rymd efter sort of guid Rob Steine." Why should such a curious importation of a foreign fashion be connected with an obscure young Edinburgh school-teacher ? The fact that Montgomerie's sonnets XLII, XLIII, are so written, though considered by Neilson "most unimportant," seems quite the opposite when one remembers that, with the exception of Stewart's verses, they are the only examples of the device in Scottish poetry of the period, and that Montgomerie is the only writer from whom we should expect such an innovation. As a third recurrence of the name, we have the King's use of it in the present poem, in the same connection, and as a jest with some hidden meaning. It may be noted incidentally that the payment to Stevin was made during the short period when Montgomerie was deprived of his pension. The use of such an alias for satirical or other purposes would of course have a multitude of parallels in poetry of all periods ; one need go for an example no further than the King's *William Mow* in the present poem. In any case, the discovery of an individual by the name of

Rob Stevin does not altogether solve the problem. What was its humorous significance? And why applied so often to Montgomerie?

In short, it is by no means certain, after all, that the latter was not the author of the *Dreme*. The style of the satire is marked by a command of language and meter equal to his own; the fulsome, oddly introduced praise of Montgomerie as "poet laureatt" is itself suspicious, especially since such 'cracking' is not out of keeping with his character and occurs in his admitted work (cf. sonnets LXII, LXVII). Montgomerie's sonnets of complaint, like the *Dreme*, are full of praise of the King and attacks on his councilors. Furthermore, we know that the poet fell from open favor at a period following Maitland's appointment to the chancellorship; whatever the cause of his downfall, it would be shrewd and characteristic of him to shift the blame from the King himself to his chief adviser.

107. *Christian Lindsay.* There are two references to this poetess in the sonnets of Montgomerie; one in the title of sonnet **XXX**, supposedly written by *Christen Lyndesay to Ro. Hudsone;* the other in sonnet **XXV**, *To R. Hudsone:* —

> " Ye can pen out tua cuple an ye pleis;
> Yourself and I, old Scot and Robert Semple.
> Quhen we ar dead, that all our dayis bot daffis,
> Let Christan Lyndesay wryt our epitaphis."

In the *Edinburgh Commissariat Records*, February 17, 1596, "Christian Lindsay, spouse to John of Dunrod, sheriff of Lanark," is so mentioned in the probate of her husband's will. John Lindsay of Dunrod was knighted at the baptism of Prince Henry (Nichols, *Prog. of Eliz.*, Vol. III, p. 368). He was later appointed one of the 'Octavians' in charge of the treasury, and reported as about to go abroad, March 5, 1597, on account of his health. (*Cal. of Border Papers*, Vol. II, p. 274.)

111. *Forder then the creede.* Beyond belief.

112. *William Mow.* A pseudonym probably suggested by *mow* = to mock, or make mouths; but *Mow* as a family

name appears not infrequently in contemporary records. It may be noted that the inverted initials of this name, M. W., are signed to one of the prefatory sonnets in *The Essayes of a Prentise* (cf. Introd., p. xxxix).

112. *Lawing.* Literally, a tavern bill or reckoning. Here applied to the evening period of recreation.

113. *Propine.* An offering or gift. It is derived from the Greek verb προπίνειν = to pledge, or drink a health, and is thus properly connected here with drinking.

LII

Mr. Rait, in printing the poem in *Lusus Regius*, failed to note that it had already appeared in *The Essayes of a Prentise*, where it immediately precedes the *Reulis and cautelis*. In view of the actual source of the poem, however, his quotation from *Ecclesiastes* i. 7, is interesting: "All the rivers run into the sea; yet the sea is not full; unto the place from whence the rivers come, thither they return again." In the *Essayes*, James quotes the following passage from Lucan, *De Bello Civili*, Bk. V, ll, 335–340: —

" Cæsaris an cursus vestræ sentire putatis
  Damnum posse fugæ? Veluti si cuncta minentur
  Flumina, quos miscent pelago, subducere fontes:
  Non magis ablatis umquam descenderet æquor,
  Quam nunc crescit, aquis. An vos momenta putatis
  Ulla dedissi mihi? "

LIII

The heading in the Maitland MS., *The King's verses when he was fyfteene yeere old,* places the date of the poem prior to June 19, 1582. The stanza in which it is written is the so-called *Commoun verse* mentioned in the *Reulis and cautelis* (cf. XVIII, note). In Calderwood, the *Antithesis* (App. II, I) follows the poem as printed here; but its admonitory tone and its omission from the Maitland and the Museum MSS. raise some doubt as to its authorship. The sententious vein of both pieces is one of the commonest in Scottish poetry of the Chaucerian tradition, though perhaps closer to Dunbar's *Ane his awin Ennemy, In Asking sowld Discretioun be,* etc., than to anything in Montgomerie.

LIV

George Gordon, sixth Earl of Huntly, and Lady Henrietta Stuart, daughter of the first Duke of Lennox, were married by Archbishop Adamson in the chapel of Holyrood Palace, July 21, 1588. Huntly had been given 5000 merks to bring his bride over from France, and received from the King as part of the wedding dowry the Abbey of Dunfermline taken from Gray (Melville, *Memoirs,* Bann. Club, p. 361). On November 28, he supplanted Glamis as Captain of the Guard, and the young couple remained with the King in Holyrood until the discovery of the 'Spanish blanks' in February revealed Huntly's bargainings with Spain. Though he made some pretense of conversion at the time of his marriage, the Earl had been and remained the chief noble of the Catholic party in Scotland. For him, says Lang (*Hist. of Scot.,* Vol. II, p. 343), James had "one of his tender fondnesses," but it should be recognized that the favor was due in large part to the King's affection for his kinswoman, the daughter of d'Aubigny. When the English agent Fowler reproached James for his clemency towards Huntly, he replied that it was "for the friendship of a young lady his daughter, and beloved of his bluid." (*Papers of Gray,* Bann. Club, p. 168, T. Fowler to Burleigh, June 22, 1589.) The Countess later frequently interceded for her husband at court, and, on his flight and the forfeiture of his estates in February, 1593, retained his principal castle, the Bog of Gicht, for her winter residence. (Tytler, *Hist. of Scot.,* Vol. IX, p. 7.)

The *Epithalamion* consists of verses for a masque or entertainment accompanied by games and brilliant spectacles, which the King devised to celebrate the wedding. Since the time was summer, these festivities no doubt were held in the garden at the back of the palace. After the speech of the King (ll. 1–34), Mercury appeared with a glittering train of fauns, sylvans, naiads, nymphs, and other spirits of the forest. The sonnet (ll. 61–74) is the challenge of the masked tilters, who now rode forward in the incongruous disguise of fauns and satyrs. The masque proper followed the tilting and probably took place indoors in the evening. The lady with her attendants approached the King seated in state at the end of the hall (l. 86), and was there addressed by her rival suitors. The numbering of the speeches would seem to indicate that only a portion of this dialogue has been preserved.

The management of the dialogue commendably illustrates the King's precepts on this matter in the *Reulis and cautelis*. "Ye man lykewayis tak heid," he writes, "that ye waill your wordis according to the purpose: as in ane heich and learnit purpose to use heich, pithie, and learnit wordis. Gif your purpose be of love, To use commoun language, with some passionate wordis. Gif your purpose be of tragicall materis, To use lamentable wordis, with some heich, as ravishit in admiratioun. Gif your purpose be of landwart effairis, To use corrupit, and uplandis wordis. And finally, quhatsumever be your subject, to use *vocabula artis*, quhairby ye may the mair vivelie represent that persoun quhais pairt ye paint out." Thus *Agrestis* speaks a broader dialect than the rest; the soldier uses "lamentable wordis, with some heich"; and the claims of all four candidates are suited to their callings.

11–30. *Thalasse, Volumna*, etc. The attributes of these for the most part obscure Roman gods and goddesses of marriage, childbirth, and nurture are as a rule sufficiently indicated by their names and by the context. With the exceptions of Prosa and Egeria, goddesses of childbirth, and Thalasse (Thalassios, another name for Hymen), they are all found in St. Augustine's *De Civitate Dei*, Bk. IV, 11–21, and were probably, as Rait suggests, taken directly from this source or from a list in some Latin grammar.

16. *Revive againe a blest and happie seede.* In answer to

the prayer, the couple were blessed with a family of five sons and four daughters.

17. *Vitumnus and Sentinus.* Gods who endow infants with life and senses. "Ibi sunt et duo nescio qui obscurissimi, Vitumnus et Sentinus, quorum alter vitam, alter sensum puerperio largiuntur." (*De Civ. Dei*, Bk. VII, 2. — Quoted in Rait.)

21. *Levana.* The goddess invoked by the parent on first lifting an infant in his arms.

23. *Vagitanus.* St. Aug., *Vaticanus.* The god who presided over a child's first cry.

25. *Cunina.* The protectress of cradles.

27. *Rumina, with Edusa, and Potina.* Deities who presided respectively over the nursing of infants, their food, and their drink.

29. *Statilinus.* Protector of infants in their first efforts to walk alone.

41. *The whisler Pan.* The King himself is celebrated as the god of shooting and singing in Ben Jonson's masque, *Pan's Anniversary.* Cf. *Hymn I :* —

> "Of Pan we sing, the best of singers, Pan,
> That taught us swains how first to tune our lays,
>
> .   .   .   .
>
> Of Pan we sing, the best of hunters, Pan,
> That drives the hart to seek unused ways."

46. *The horne of Amalthœe.* Cornucopia or horn of plenty. An allusion to the goat's horn filled with fresh herbs and fruit presented by the nymph Amalthea to the infant Zeus. According to another version of the legend, the deity broke off one of the horns of the goat and gave it to his nurses, endowing it with the power of becoming filled with whatever the possessor might wish.

48. *Glove, or ring.* Though the *N.E.D.* is doubtful on the subject, the glove was clearly used, like rings, as a target for a spearsman on horseback. Cf. Marlowe's *Tamburlaine*, Pt. II, I, iii, 39 : —

> "Trotting the ring, and tilting at a glove."

In *A True Accompt . . . of the Baptism of . . . Prince Henry*, Edinburgh, [1594], written probably by William Fowler (Nichols, *Progresses of Eliz.*, Vol. III, pp. 353-369), there is a description of an entertainment, similar to this one, at Stirling Castle, which "devided both in field-pastimes with martiall and heroicall exploits, and in house-hold with rare shewes and singular inventions." There was "running at the ring and glove," in which the contestants, led by the King, were three Knights of Malta, three Amazons, and three Moors, all masked.

55. *Allridge.* Elfish.

60. *Wa.* Will.

60. *What racks essaye and see.* What harm to make a trial. *Racks* is a form of the verb *reck* = to take heed or take care.

65. *Sume does your Court, to Arthurs court compare.* The comparison was made later by Walter Quin, an Irish scholar and teacher of languages, who wrote a sonnet on the subject, *Charles James Stuart claims Arthurs Seat.* (Preserved in the Records Office with other sonnets, Latin epigrams, anagrams on the King's name, etc., by the same author. Cf. *Cal. S. P. Sco.*, p. 701.) Though the title plays upon the name of the hill overlooking Holyrood, the poem deals chiefly with James's resemblance to his illustrious ancestor. An anonymous letter to Bowes (*Ibid.*, December 4, 1595) speaks of the "arrival of Walter Quin, an Irishman, learned, courtly and well traveled, who has been with the King divers times and given him a treatise of poesie. Since these verses were exhibited to the King, what with speaking with the man, and what by the sending of the verses, and the bruit arrived of the Spaniards, the King has become incredibly rejoiced." For further account of Quin, cf. Introd., p. xxxviii.

89. *kappit.* Entrapped, possessed. Cf. *Demonologie*, Bk. II, c. 6 : — "Yet to these capped creatures, he appears as he pleases, and as he findes meetest for their humors." (Rait.)

92. *Zanie.* Clown. A diminutive of the Ital. *Giovanni*.

98. *Sillie.* Simple. It has been pointed out that when

the irascible preacher Andrew Melville took James by the sleeve in Holyrood Palace and called him "God's sillie vassal" (J. Melville's *Diary*, Bann. Club, p. 245, October, 1596), he was probably using the adjective in its milder meaning.

100. *Tine.* Lose.

LV

For an account of the voyage to Denmark and the King's marriage, cf. note on the *Amatoria*, pp. 69–71.

3. *Ethnicks.* Pagans. The phrasing and thought of the passage are recalled in Montgomerie's *Epitaphe of Johne and Patrik Shaues*, ll. 1–4 : —

"If ethnik ald by superstitious stylis,
Quhilk poyson yit of Paganisme appeirs,
Wer stellified to rule the rolling spheirs,
As Paganism [pagan ?] poets and profane compylis," etc.

10. *Stounde.* Moment.

20. *Rod.* A not uncommon Scottish spelling of *road.* (*N.E.D.*)

25. *Redounding.* Overflowing, abundant.

32. James probably changed the original phrasing to avoid the suggestion of limited power in the word *tyed.* Cf. the reading in Rait (footnote).

33–36. *And lacking parents*, etc. The passage is reminiscent of *The Kingis Majesteis Declaratioun upoun the Causis of His Departur* (*Papers relative to the Marriage of King James the Sixth*, Bann. Club, p. 12 ff.) : "As to the causes, I doubt nochte it is manifestlie knowne to all how far I wes generallie found fault with be all men for the delaying sa lang of my marriage ; the ressonis wer, that I wes allane, without fader or moder, brouthir or sister, king of this realme and air appeirand of England ; this my naikitnes maid me to be waik and my Inemyis to be stark, ane man wes as na man, and the want of hoip of succession bread disdayne." The last "King that was a man" in Scotland was James's grandfather, James V, who died in 1542.

35. *Kitle.* Difficult to deal with, 'ticklish.' The King
in his letter to the council sought to convince them that his
journey was not rash or dangerous, considering "the schorte-
nes of the way, the suretie of the passage, being clene of all
sandis, foirlandis, or siclike dangeiris, the harboreyis in these
partis sa suir, and na forreyne fleetis resorting upoun these
seis. It is my plesure then that na man grudge or murmour
at thir my procedingis."

LVI

For an account of the relations of James and Du Bartas,
cf. Introd., p. xxxiv. In the 1593 edition of Du Bartas (*La
Sepmaine ou Creation du Monde*, de Guillaume De Sallust,
seigneur du Bartas, Paris, 1593), which is the earliest to
which I have had access, the passage translated occurs not
in the first 'day,' but in the *Second Jour de la [première]
semaine*, ll. 41–107. The translation is almost line for line
and very close, save that the unfortunately long meter
which James has chosen necessitates frequent padding with
adjectives. The conceitfulness and grotesqueness of style,
however, is if anything less than in the original. Even
James would have hesitated to suggest, for instance, that
the word of God was "syringué" into chaos. A comparison of the first six lines with the same passage in Du
Bartas will be sufficient to illustrate James's method : —

" Ceste longue largeur, ceste hauteur profonde,
Cest infini fini, ce grande monde sans monde,
Ce lourd (di-je) Chaos, qui dans soi mutiné,
Se vid en un moment dans le rien d'un rienné,
Estoit le corps fecond d'où la celeste essence
Et les quatre Elemens devoyent prendre naissance."

3. *lourde.* Heavy.
11. *Now. Whether*, the original reading, is a better translation of Du Bartas's *soit que*, which begins both this line
and the second following.
16. *Acheloian sucke.* Water. *Achelous* was the name

of the largest river in Greece and of the river-god who fought with Hercules.

18. *Chilus.* Chyle. The juice formed in the stomach by the digestion of food. "Il se prend pour le seu que le ventricule tire des viandes par le moyen de la digestion, et qui est la matière du sang." — Note by S.G.S. (Sieur Guillaume Sallust ?) in Du Bartas.

23. *Like warre dothe holde our bod' in peace.* Here follows an explanation of the complexions, melancholy, sanguine, phlegmatic, and choleric, resultant from the divers combinations of the elements in the human body. Rait quotes in illustration the *Counterblaste to Tobacco* (1616 Folio, p. 216): "For man beeing compounded of the foure Complexions, although there be a mixture of them all in all the parts of his body, yet must the divers parts of our *Microcosme*, or little world within ourselves, be diversly more inclined, some to one, some to another complexion, according to the diversitie of their uses, that of these discords a perfect harmonie may be made up for the maintenance of the whole body."

41. *Citties Democratick free.* In 1603 James told Scaravelli, the Secretary of the Venetian Embassy, of "the days . . . when my tutor, Buchanan, gave me instruction in the excellence of that government [the Venetian Republic]." — *S. P. Ven.*, Vol. X, No. 78. Here, however, the passage is a direct translation.

50. Cf. Du Bartas, l. 90 : —

"Se fait moust, le moust vin, et le bon vin vinaigre."

55. *Bot if that cruell Tyranne like.* The question of the right of the people to rebel against an oppressive monarch was a moot point in the political discussions of the sixteenth century. Buchanan, in *De Jure Regni apud Scotos*, sought to justify tyrannicide.

56. *Saickles.* Innocent.

61. *Affeirand.* Properly appertaining to each other. Du Bartas : —

"Une proportion conjoint, bien qu'inegales."

67. *Boore bot one craig*, etc. The wish ascribed by Suetonius to Caligula: "Utinam populus Romanus unam cervicem haberet." (*De Vita Cæsarum*, IV, c. 30.)

69. The translation ends suddenly, but with discretion. The next lines in Du Bartas are as follows: —

"De tous ses compagnons il cerche la ruine:
Peu à peu la maison, où tyran il domine,
Ruyneuse se perd: et dedans et dehors,
Aux yeux plus cler-voyans semble changer de corps."

LVII

The translation is from *La Seconde Sepmaine, Premier Jour*, ll. 1–48, and is as close as the one preceding.

4. *Crooked.* The verb. Du Bartas, *serpentoit*.

6. *From Edens both.* Du Bartas, *les deux Edens*. The terrestrial and celestial paradises, both closed by Adam's fall.

11. *Leste.* To extend or last. Du Bartas, *allongeant mon propos*.

13. *Marche.* Limit, boundary.

15. *Droucked.* Du Bartas, *toute moite*. Drenched or wet. Cf. Douglas, *Æneis*, Bk. X, vi, ll. 44–45: —

". . . All droukit and forwrocht,
They salffit war, and warpit to the cost."

17. *O sacred floure du lis.* A reference to Henry, King of Navarre (1553–1610), son of Antoine de Bourbon and Jeanne d'Albret. He became Henry IV of France in 1589.

20. *And helpe the faults rise.* Faults (Sc. *faultis*) is dissyllabic.

21. *Pampelone.* Sp. Pamplona. The ancient capital city of Navarre, seized with the greater portion of the kingdom by Ferdinand of Castile in 1512.

27. *Fighting at thy side.* Du Bartas was a soldier as well as diplomatist and poet; he died of wounds received while fighting under Henry in the battle of Ivry (May 14, 1590).

36. *Bricole.* Du Bartas, *vont bricollant.* To bound or rebound; a technical term used especially in tennis.

39. *With variant ameling paimented.* Paved or covered with varied decoration. Cf. XIII, 8; XVII, 177.

43. *Adjourned.* Du Bartas, *semond.* Here in the unusual sense of *summoned.*

APPENDIX I

III

The phrase "sonnets and suites to the Gods," in the opening sentence, has reference to twelve sonnets at the beginning of *The Essayes of a Prentise*, three of which, with a four-line introduction, are reprinted in the present volume (XLI–XLIV). The *Scheme* itself is apparently an ingenious outline for a poem which should illustrate the "kyndis of verses" defined in Chapter VIII of the *Reulis and cautelis.* The portion preceding the delivery of the bill to the Gods was to be in *rithme* [*rhyme*], by which James probably meant couplets — either decasyllabics or 'fourteeners.' The Muses then request an answer in *ballet royall*, described by James in the *Reulis* as a stanza of eight lines rhyming *ababbcbc.* Envy opposes in *tragicall verse*, presumably *Troilus verse* or *rhyme royal*, recommended by James for tragical matters and complaints. Jupiter strikes a *midds* or mean between the contending parties in *heroicall verse*, a stanza rhyming *aab, aab, bab;* and the piece closes with a sonnet.

APPENDIX II

I

In Calderwood the *Antithesis* follows and forms a part of the *Song, the first verses that ever the King made* (LIII). See note on the latter poem.

II

The Spanish fleet was defeated in July, 1588, and a portion driven northward around Scotland. During the flight one of the vessels was stranded on the coast of Anstruther, and the crew entertained by the natives with kail, porridge, and fish (Melville's *Diary*, p. 174). Medina de Sidonia, who was in the party, visited Edinburgh and probably saw the King. Hence line 11 of the sonnet: —

"The number that escap'd, it fell them faire."

III

Cf. *A Sonnet to Chanceller Maitlane* (XXXIII), and note.

IV

The omission of the sonnet in the second and later editions of the treatise may be attributed not only to its inferiority to the sonnet following, but to its departure in the first quatrain from the King's usual rhyme-scheme.

V

This piece has been highly praised. J. H. Millar calls it "by far his best performance . . . which just misses being really fine." (*A Literary History of Scotland*, N.Y., 1903, p. 214.)

10. *Represse the proud*, etc. Cf. the King's motto: "Parcere subiectis et debellare superbos."

VI–VII

The date of these verses is indicated by a letter from John Chamberlain to Sir Dudley Carleton, August 18, 1621 (Nichols, *Progresses of James I*, Vol. IV, p. 710): "The King was so pleased and taken with his entertainment at the Lord Marquess's, that he could not forbear to express his contentment in certain verses he made to this effect, that 'the air, the weather (though it was not so here), and every thing else, even the stags and bucks in their fall did seem to smile; so that there was hopes of a smiling boy within a while,' to which end he concluded with a wish, or *votum*, for the felicity and fruitfulness of that virtuous and blessed couple, and in a way of Amen, caused the Bishop of London in his presence to give them a blessing." The latter ceremony is presumably indicated by the asterisks, VII, 7. The marriage of Buckingham and Lady Katherine Manners took place May 16, 1620, and their first child, a daughter, was born in April, 1622 (*Ibid.*, p. 756). During his visit, which extended from July 29 to August 4, the King was entertained with Ben Jonson's *Masque of the Metamorphosed Gypsies*, which so pleased him that it was performed twice again, at Belvoir and Windsor, in the same month. This was the occasion also of Sir John Beaumont's sonnets, *Of his Maiestie's Vow for the Felicity of my Lord Marquesse of Buckingham* and *My Lord of Buckingham's Welcome to the King at Burley* (*Poems*, ed. Grosart, pp. 156–157).

INDEX